STUFF EVERY
TEA LOVER
SHOULD KNOW

STUFF EVERY

TEA LOVER

SHOULD KNOW

Candace Rose Rardon

QUIRK BOOKS

PHILADELPHIA

*To my mother Janell—for all our
delightful mornings at Smithfield Bakery,
sharing pots of English breakfast and scones*

Library of Congress Cataloging in Publication Number: 2019955183

ISBN: 978-1-68369-178-5

Printed in China

Typeset in Laca, Brandon Grotesque, Adobe Garamond, and Akzidenz-Grotesk

Cover design by Elissa Flanigan
Interior design by Molly Rose Murphy
Illustrations by Lucy Engelman
Production management by John J. McGurk

Quirk Books
215 Church Street
Philadelphia, PA 19106
quirkbooks.com
10 9 8 7 6 5 4 3 2 1

TEA FAMILIES & COMMON VARIETIES

TEA TRADITIONS ACROSS THE WORLD

TEA PARTIES

INTRODUCTION

"Would you like an adventure now, or would you like to have your tea first?"

—J. M. BARRIE, *PETER PAN*

Since its discovery nearly five thousand years ago, tea has become the second most widely consumed beverage in the world (after water). As a travel writer and artist, I've spent the past decade traveling through more than fifty countries, and as I've journeyed around the world, there has always been a cup of tea by my side. Whether in England, India, or the countryside of Turkey, people have opened their homes to me, offered me tea in a dazzling range of flavors, shapes, and styles, and taught me how to prepare tea—and share it—according to their rituals and traditions. Across the globe, I've found there's something to learn from even the smallest cup of tea.

Here are a few reasons that help explain tea's universal appeal.

- **Tea calms us.** What is more comforting than curling up under a cozy blanket with a good book and a hot cup of tea? This soothing beverage makes us feel more at home, no matter where we are in the world.

- **Tea is good for us.** More than twenty amino acids and antioxidants are found in tea leaves; one of them is theanine, which is known for calming and relaxing the mind. For thousands of years, the many health benefits of tea have made it the ultimate form of self-care—a nourishing brew for body and soul.

- **Tea connects us.** If you've ever wandered the bustling markets of Marrakech, Istanbul, or Delhi, friendly vendors have undoubtedly offered you a glass of mint tea or masala chai before they laid out a single ware. In countless cultures, tea is a tangible symbol of hospitality, kindness, and connection. Tea brings people together—helping us not only savor each moment, but share those moments with others. And so in the pages to come, even as we focus on practical how-tos like brewing methods and tea tastings, may this deeper "why" always be at the heart of the book.

As we'll soon discover, tea has many stories to tell. This book is my humble attempt to honor the incredible and complex role that tea has played in cultures across the globe. In many ways it only scratches the surface, but I hope it will help you on your journey as a tea lover, guiding you in new directions to explore.

TEA
BASICS

WHAT IS TEA?

There's a legend dating the history of tea to the year 2737 BCE. It opens with the revered Chinese emperor Shen Nung, a mythical hero and avid herbalist who was known as the Divine Healer. The details of the legend are recounted differently from version to version, but they all agree that one day, as Shen Nung boiled water to drink, a few leaves fell from a wild tea bush into his pot below. Anyone who has ever submerged a tea bag in hot water knows what happened next: the world's first pot of tea was inadvertently brewed.

The leaves that led to Shen Nung's serendipitous discovery of tea fell from a small evergreen shrub called *Camellia sinensis*. One of the most remarkable things to know about tea is that all six true tea families are made from this one species of tea plant. These six families are:

WHITE	GREEN	YELLOW
OOLONG	BLACK	DARK

Once the leaves of the tea plant have been harvested and processed (we'll talk more about this soon), tea is created when the leaves combine with hot water to make an infusion, which is a drink prepared by soaking the leaves of a plant in liquid. However, although tea is an infusion, not all infusions are tea. For instance, popular medicinal teas such as peppermint or chamomile aren't technically tea, because they aren't derived from the *Camellia sinensis* plant; rather, these are herbal infusions. Any infusion not produced using tea leaves is also referred to as a *tisane*.

But by no means has this distinction between "true teas" and other infusions limited the evolution of the hot drink. Perhaps more than any other beverage in the world, tea has been shaped into a myriad of forms and flavors, which even the most dedicated of tea lovers could spend a lifetime exploring.

HIGHLIGHTS FROM TEA HISTORY

"I am glad I was not born before tea."
—SYDNEY SMITH

A lot has happened in the world of tea over five thousand years—even the English name for tea was an evolution. Most of China called it *cha*, but the first Dutch traders who carried tea to Europe brought it from the port of Amoy in Fujian Province, where tea was known as *tê* in the local dialect. Here are some more defining moments that helped shape the course and culture of our favorite hot drink.

Prehistory: In the *Illustrated Encyclopedia of Prehistoric Man* (first published in 1975 in French), Jan Jelínek shares archaeological evidence suggesting that man boiled tea leaves from the *Camellia sinensis* plant as far back as the Paleolithic age, the earliest period of human development, in the area that is modern-day China.

2737 BCE: According to Chinese legend, emperor Shen Nung discovers tea and becomes the first proponent of its medicinal benefits.

7th century CE: By the T'ang dynasty, tea is an everyday part of life in China. Also at this time, Buddhist monks from Korea and Japan begin traveling to China for religious studies, returning home with tea seeds and thereby helping spur the spread of tea across Asia.

780: T'ang dynasty tea master Lu Yu publishes the world's first treatise on tea, *The Classic of Tea*.

10th century: The ancient Tea Horse Road is established, ushering in centuries of trade between China and Tibet in which Chinese tea is exchanged for Tibetan horses. Tea is such a valuable commodity at this time that it becomes a form of currency, with the price for horses sometimes given in tea bricks.

1391: Ming dynasty emperors prohibit compressed teas, which were molded into bricks or cakes. This leads to innovations in tea production, such as the creation of loose-leaf tea, which requires less work to process than cake teas. As Ming dynasty scholar Ye Ziqi observes, "Leaf tea is everywhere."

1500s: The new Chinese method of steeping loose tea in hot water leads to new tea vessels, namely the world's first teapots, crafted from clay in the city of Yixing. Black and oolong tea production also begins in Fujian Province.

1580s: Renowned tea master Sen no Rikyū greatly refines the Japanese tea ceremony, establishing principles and traditions that remain unchanged today.

1606: The first known shipment of tea arrives in Europe, sent by the Dutch East India Company from China to Amsterdam.

1657: The Dutch bring tea to London for the first time. The next year, Thomas Garraway purchases the first newspaper ad for tea in England, and in 1660, famed English diarist Samuel Pepys records: "I did send for a Cupp of Tee (a China drink) of which I never had drank before . . ."

1662: King Charles II of England marries Portuguese princess Catherine of Braganza, who helps make tea fashionable among the British upper class.

1717: Thomas Twining opens his first tea house in London.

1773: The Boston Tea Party is held as a political protest by American colonists against high taxes imposed upon them by the British government.

1823: Scottish trader Robert Bruce discovers native tea plants in India. This is a key turning point for the

British, who are keen to grow less reliant on China for tea.

1839–1858: The Opium Wars mark one of the darkest moments in the history of tea, as Britain's huge demand for the drink is a key impetus for both wars. In order to pay for vast quantities of Chinese tea, the British East India Company begins trading opium with China—and they refuse to stop, even when the Chinese emperor makes opium illegal out of concern for the alarming number of people in his country who've become addicted. As a result, England goes to war twice with China, and both times the Chinese suffer devastating losses. As BBC correspondent Justin Rowlatt wrote in a 2016 article, the Opium Wars "could just as well be called the Tea Wars."

1848: In response to the Chinese keeping their tea-growing secrets under lock and key, Scottish botanist and so-called tea thief Robert Fortune is sent by the British East India Company to China, and he manages to smuggle 20,000 tea plants—and growing techniques—back to India.

1858: British colonial rule in India is established, giving Britain the ability to grow their own tea and gradually lessen their dependence on China.

1908: A New York tea importer named Thomas Sullivan sends out samples of loose tea to his customers in silk bags, unintentionally inventing the tea bag.

1987: The Charleston Tea Plantation is founded in South Carolina, making it the first large-scale commercial tea estate in North America. Their American Classic Tea is the only tea brand made entirely from U.S.-grown tea leaves.

TERMS EVERY TEA LOVER SHOULD KNOW

Aroma: The scent of both brewed tea leaves and the tea liquor; also referred to as the *nose*.

Astringency: The feeling of dryness in the mouth caused by tannins; more oxidized teas tend to have greater astringency.

Body: The consistency and texture of a tea's liquor, often classified as light-, medium-, or full-bodied; also known as *mouthfeel*.

Bud: The unopened leaf bud (not a flower bud) on a tea plant, whose pointed, tightly furled appearance is often compared to the shape of a sword or sparrow's tongue; *budset* refers to the bud when it is plucked with one or two leaves.

Camellia sinensis: The species of evergreen plant from which all six true tea families are made. Native to China, India, and other regions in southeast Asia, it thrives in tropical and subtropical climates and today is cultivated around the world.

Character: The distinctive nature and qualities of a tea, including its aroma, flavor, and appearance, given its growing country or region.

CTC method: Short for "cut, tear, curl," this term refers to the mechanical method for producing lesser-quality black tea. Ninety percent of black tea produced today is made using this method and used in tea bags to make a strong, quick brew.

Finish: The lingering flavor of tea on the palate.

Flush: A period during which tea leaves are growing and ready for plucking; *first flush* refers to the first harvest of the year.

Hui gan: This Chinese phrase meaning "returning sweetness" is used to describe teas with a long finish.

Liquor: The liquid tea produced by steeping tea leaves in water.

Orthodox method: The traditional method for manufacturing whole-leaf black tea, often by hand.

Oxidation: The chemical reaction that occurs when enzymes in the tea leaf are exposed to oxygen, which is either encouraged or prevented during production depending on the desired style of tea.

Plucking: The action of picking buds and leaves from the tea plant.

Sachets: Higher-quality tea bags often shaped like a pyramid (to give tea leaves more room to unfurl as they brew) and containing loose-leaf or long-leaf tea, rather than lower-grade fannings (see page 71).

Single-garden: Term used to describe tea produced by one garden or estate, rather than a blend of teas from multiple estates.

Terroir: French term for "a sense of place" that refers to the mix of environmental and physical factors that influence a tea's character, such as the climate, weather, soil, topography, etc.

Theanine: Amino acid found in tea leaves known for calming the mind without causing drowsiness; along with other polyphenols, it also helps slow the body's absorption of caffeine.

Theine: The name originally given to the caffeine found in tea. Although it was proved in 1838 that theine and caffeine are the same substance, *theine* is still used as a term when talking about tea.

Tisane: Herbal tea or infusion not produced with leaves from the *Camellia sinensis* plant.

ANATOMY OF THE TEA PLANT

From young, tender leaf buds to the more mature lower leaves, each part of the tea plant plays a role in tea production and is used to make specific varieties of tea. Let's take a closer look at the almighty *Camellia sinensis*.

Bud: Used for premium teas such as Silver Needle white tea (see page 80).

Second and third leaves: Used for higher-grade teas.

Budset: The bud plucked with one or two leaves, used for a range of teas, including Jasmine Pearls green tea (see page 77), Keemun black tea (see page 67), and White Peony white tea (see page 80).

Fourth and fifth leaves: Used for oolong and some black teas such as Lapsang souchong (see page 66), which require more processing.

Stem: Used to make *kukicha* twig tea in Japan (see page 76).

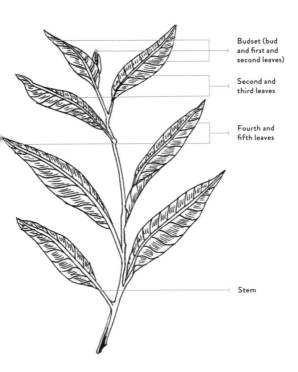

Budset (bud and first and second leaves)

Second and third leaves

Fourth and fifth leaves

Stem

HOW TEA IS MADE

*"I am in no way interested in immortality,
but only in the taste of tea."*

—LU T'UNG, NINTH-CENTURY CHINESE POET

The journey of every type of tea—whether we're talking about a sweet Silver Needle white, a grassy Sencha green, or an earthy *pu-erh*—begins at the same moment: when fresh leaves are plucked from the *Camellia sinensis* plant. A tea's final identity is shaped by what happens to the leaves *after* they're harvested, and it all has to do with oxidation.

This process, also known as enzymatic browning, is one you're no doubt familiar with. If you've ever peeled an apple or avocado and watched it turn brown as it's exposed to the air, that's the power of oxidation. And if you've ever baked an apple in the oven and watched the browning stop, that's the power of heat to *disrupt* the process of oxidation.

Oxygen and heat—these are the fundamental players at the heart of tea production. Other possible steps include withering, rolling, fixing, and drying. This brief overview outlines how these processes help create the six different families of tea.

WHITE TEA

As the least processed category of tea, white teas are the minimalists of the tea world, undergoing only two processing steps. The first and most important step for white tea is *withering*. After the leaves are plucked, they're spread into thin layers—either indoors or under the sun—to begin drying out. The next step is *drying*; the leaves' moisture content is reduced further, often in a hot air dryer at a low temperature, to just 2 to 3 percent.

GREEN TEA

Think of each family of tea as building on the last. Green tea adds another step to the process: *fixing*. Green tea is zero percent oxidized, because the leaves are fixed with heat (like the apple in the oven) after a short period of withering to prevent enzymes in the tea leaves from oxidizing. Fixing is also referred to as *de-enzyming* or *denaturing*; in Chinese, this step is known as *sha qing*, which literally means "killing the green." Fixing can look different depending on the country. In China tea leaves are often pan-fired in large woks; Japanese green teas are steamed. Other fixing methods exist, all of which result in green teas with strikingly distinct flavors and aromas.

YELLOW TEA

Yellow tea undergoes nearly the same process as green tea, but for the addition of one important step. After being briefly fixed, the leaves are wrapped, typically in either cloth or paper. Known in Chinese as *men huan*, or "sealing yellow," this step is unique to yellow teas and has a number of names in English—*wrapping*, *smothering*, and *sweltering*, to name a few. No matter the name, the result is the same: wrapping the leaves causes a mild fermentation (as opposed to dark teas, which are fully fermented) that softens the tea's astringency and gives yellow tea its characteristic mellow taste.

OOLONG TEA

If white teas are minimalists, oolongs are high maintenance, requiring more work than any other type of tea. With oolong we finally arrive at the families of tea where oxidation is encouraged. Oolong tea is semi-oxidized, putting it on the processing spectrum between green and black teas. Varieties of oolong may be oxidized as little as 5 to 10 percent or as much as 70 to 80 percent. (Note: these percentages refer to the amount of oxygen the tea leaves have absorbed; the oxygen then reacts with certain enzymes in the leaves and causes changes in a tea's flavor and color.)

Oolong teas are also special for how they're oxidized, via a process known as *bruising*. In Chinese this step is called *yao qing* (literally "rocking the green"), and this name refers to how the leaves are shaken and tossed after withering. This bruises the edges of the leaves, exposing their enzymes to more oxygen.

BLACK TEA

Known in Chinese as *hong cha*, or "red tea," due to the color of its liquor, black tea is 100 percent oxidized. After the tea leaves are withered, they undergo a second step known as *rolling*. Rolling is done either by machine or (rarely) by hand, and it encourages oxidation by breaking down the leaves at a cellular level and exposing more of their enzymes to the air. Finally, the leaves are fully oxidized, giving this tea its defining bold flavors and astringency.

There are two main methods for manufacturing black tea. The orthodox method processes whole leaves by rolling them into strips. A newer method, known as CTC (short for "cut, tear, curl"), uses machines to cut the leaves into tiny, equally sized granules; this process was invented in the 1930s as a means for filling tea bags.

DARK TEA

Another reason why the Chinese refer to black tea as "red tea" is because they refer to a different family of tea as black: dark teas, such as *pu-erh*. Dark teas are the only teas that are fully fermented, and there are two ways this happens: natural or artificial fermentation, resulting in teas known as either raw or ripe. In both methods, the leaves are fixed at lower temperatures than other kinds of tea, which helps stop oxidation but doesn't kill all of the natural bacteria and yeast needed for fermentation. This is the only family of tea that gets better as it ages, like fine wine.

CAFFEINE CONTENT

An average cup of coffee has 95 milligrams of caffeine, which gives us that instant jolt of energy. Not only does tea generally contain less caffeine than coffee, but thanks to an amino acid called theanine, we also experience the caffeine in tea differently. Theanine slows down the body's absorption of caffeine, effectively "releasing" the caffeine in tea little by little and helping us feel a more sustained level of awareness than coffee provides.

TEA FAMILY	CAFFEINE CONTENT PER 8 OZ. SERVING
White tea	15–30mg
Green tea	35–45mg
Yellow tea	33mg
Oolong tea	37–55mg
Black tea	40–70mg
Dark tea	60–70mg

TEA TASTING 101

Don't know how to start appreciating tea on a deeper level? Approaching it like a wine tasting is a fun way of thinking about the breadth and depth of this beverage. There are many parallels between the two worlds.

- **Variety:** Just as one grape, *Vitis vinifera*, is the source of countless wine varietals, so do all of the world's tea cultivars descend from the single *Camellia sinensis* species.

- **Terroir:** Wine and tea are both profoundly influenced by the environment they were produced in.

- **Tannin:** This polyphenol lends its signature astringency to tea and wine alike, especially black teas and red wines.

- **Sommeliers:** Just as in the world of wine, individuals can train and become certified as professional tea sommeliers.

- **Vintage:** Fine wines and dark teas are identified by the year and place in which they were produced.

But perhaps the greatest point of connection between wine and tea is the attention required to fully appreciate them. There is so much more to observe than taste alone, from the layered notes of an aroma to the color of a particular brew—and discerning and expressing these qualities take time.

One of the goals of tea tasting is simply to put into words what you're experiencing: Is the aroma fruity or floral? Is the finish dry or round? What sets this tea apart from others? Here are ten things to evaluate when tasting a quality whole-leaf tea, organized into three stages of the tasting process—before, during, and after you've tasted a tea.

BEFORE

- Name of the tea: Before you put the kettle on, take a moment to note important details about the tea you'll be drinking—what family it belongs to, its country of production, and, for some varieties (such as Darjeeling), even the estate where the leaves were grown. Knowing these facts will also help you prepare the tea with the correct water temperature and infusion time (see chart on page 61).

- Appearance of the dry leaf: Spend time with the dry leaves before brewing, considering their color, shape, the number of buds, etc. Given the kind of tea it is, does it look like it should? For example, if you're preparing a Silver Needle white tea, do the buds have their defining downy hairs? Or if it's an oolong tea, are the leaves closer in color to green or black? The dry leaf has a lot to tell you about how the tea was processed and oxidized.

- Aroma of the dry leaf: A huge part of a tea's flavor in fact has to do with its aromas, starting with the scent of the dry leaves. For an even richer sensory experience, pick up a few of the leaves, bring them close to your ear, and roll them between your fingers—if you hear a crunching sound, this means the leaves are fresh.

> Tip: Show off those leaves. When you're host-ing a tea tasting with friends, don't forget to set out some of the dry leaves for their aroma and appearance to be appreciated. You could place the leaves on a small plate or bowl, or use a *cha he*—a Chinese tea presentation vessel.

DURING

- Aroma and appearance of the wet leaf: As the leaves absorb the hot water and are rehydrated, their aroma notes change considerably. Study the leaves just after they've been infused, comparing the aromas of the dry and wet leaves. Vegetal notes detected at this stage indicate a fresh tea. The infused leaves can sometimes tell you more about the tea than the taste of the liquor itself.

- Aroma of the liquor: A 1977 study found that 80 percent of the flavors we perceive as taste come from what we smell, so it's no surprise we should smell the infused tea before we taste it. For this step, it's helpful to use an *aroma cup*, which resembles a tall, oversized thimble. To use, pour the tea first into the aroma cup, then immediately into your tasting cup—the empty aroma cup allows you to focus solely on how the liquor smells.

- Color of the liquor: Next, take a moment to study the color of the liquor, such as the pale tones of green tea or the rich, coppery reds of black tea. Is the liquor shining and clear? Even the darkest teas should have a sparkling translucence, rather than looking cloudy or murky.

- Taste of the liquor: At last, it's time to taste the tea! But our sense of smell still plays a big role here, thanks to something known as *retronasal olfaction*—which basically means we can smell food or drink from inside our mouth. To see this at work, try pinching your nose when you take a sip; much of the tea's flavor will be suddenly blocked. Now, try exhaling through your nose while you have tea in your mouth and you'll get an even fuller sense of its aromatic palate.

- **Texture of the liquor:** This step puts our sense of touch to good use. As we study how the liquor physically feels as we drink, we're evaluating its texture and mouthfeel: Is the tea rough or smooth? Silky or astringent? Creamy or robust?

Tip: Get personal. Sure, you can look up how a certain tea smells or tastes, but it's way more fun to experience these qualities for yourself. Record your own first impressions before reading someone else's opinion, and don't worry about finding the perfect descriptors right away, either—start by just thinking about what the tea reminds you of and if it conjures any memories. As Don Mei of the British tea company Mei Leaf shares in his YouTube video "How to Taste Tea (Like a Pro)": "You start to build up a personal connection with the tea. . . . You want not to describe what the tea is, but what the tea is for *you*."

AROMA EVALUATION: NAMING THE FRAGRANCE OF TEA

Think of your palate like a muscle, one that takes time to train and fine-tune. As you develop your tea-tasting skills, keep the following questions in mind.

What aroma families can you smell?

- **Vegetal:** grassy, herbal, hay
- **Fruit:** citrus, tropical, berries, even preserves and jams
- **Sweet:** honey, vanilla, malt, caramel, chocolate
- **Marine:** seaweed, kelp
- **Other scents:** smoky, spicy, nutty, or floral

How about any nonfood aromas?

- **Earthy:** damp soil, peat, moss, mushrooms
- **Woodsy:** dry wood, burning wood, pine
- **Animal:** leather, musk, wool
- **Other scents:** charcoal, minerals, stone

AFTER

- **Finish of the liquor:** How long did the flavor linger in your mouth? Did it dissipate quickly? Or was the taste persistent? Also analyze where you can still feel the tea in your mouth—on the sides of your tongue, the back of your throat, or does it have an all-around full finish? The Chinese have a special term for this quality of tea: *hui gan*, which loosely translates as "returning sweetness."

- **Tasting notes:** Be sure to take notes during each tasting, to gradually develop your vocabulary of aromas, tastes, and textures. You could even get a tea tasting journal (Moleskine makes one), many of which come with flavor wheels for visually mapping a tea's aromatic profile. With each new variety you try, your journey through the world of tea continues!

LU YU: THE PATRON SAINT OF TEA

In 780 renowned Chinese tea master Lu Yu wrote *The Classic of Tea*, the first known treatise on the beverage. Enjoy these poetic excerpts from his magnum opus.

On selecting tea leaves:

"The best quality tea must have creases like the leather boot of Tartar horsemen, curl like the dewlap of a mighty bullock, unfold like a mist rising out of a ravine, gleam like a lake touched by a zephyr, and be wet and soft like a fine earth newly swept by rain."

On boiling water for tea:

"When the water is boiling, it must look like fishes' eyes and give off but the hint of a sound. When at the edges it clatters like a bubbling spring and looks like pearls innumerable strung together, it has reached the second stage. When it leaps like breakers majestic and resounds like a swelling wave, it is at its peak."

On the benefits of tea:

"Tea tempers the spirits and harmonizes the mind, dispels lassitude and relieves fatigue, awakens thought and prevents drowsiness, lightens or refreshes the body, and clears the perceptive faculties."

TEA BAGS VS. LOOSE LEAF

"Tea! Bless ordinary everyday afternoon tea!"

—AGATHA CHRISTIE, *AND THEN THERE WERE NONE*

For much of tea's history, the debate between tea bags versus loose leaf didn't exist—loose-leaf tea was the only choice. That all changed in the 1900s, thanks to a New York tea importer named Thomas Sullivan. He routinely sent out samples of loose tea, packaged in tin canisters, to vendors and customers. One day, to save money, Sullivan started sending out the samples in silk bags, fully intending for the tea to be removed before it was brewed. To his surprise, his customers placed the bags directly in hot water and soon were asking him for more—the rest is history!

Despite their enthusiastic reception, tea bags now hold a contentious place in the world of tea, due to the quality of tea that many bags contain. Although the teas discussed throughout this book are whole leaf, let's take a moment to discuss the pros and cons of the ever-controversial tea bag.

CONS

- **Quality:** Tea bags contain the bottom of the tea-production totem pole—i.e., fannings and tea dust leftover from producing loose-leaf tea.

- **Size and shape:** Standard, flat tea bags aren't large enough to allow the leaves enough room to properly expand as the tea steeps (although new designs such as pyramid-shaped tea bags and sachets are helping to change this).

- **Flavor:** Broken tea leaves and fannings lack many of the essential oils found in whole leaves—which translates to less aroma *and* fewer antioxidants. Broken tea also releases tannins faster than whole leaves, which can lead to a more bitter taste—a flaw that's covered up by the milk and sugar often added to tea brewed from a bag.

Tip: When discussing tea's health benefits, often the focus is on the family of tea—for example, green tea over black tea. What we should be focusing on instead is the *quality*. Whole leaves, and especially buds, contain far more nutrients than the broken bits used in tea bags.

PROS

Given the downsides of tea bags, you might be inclined to swear them off forever. But let's not be too hasty to dismiss them.

- **Convenience:** When you're on the go, nothing compares to tea bags. They're easy to brew and easy to clean up.

- **Affordability:** Quality loose-leaf tea requires an investment—of both your time in preparing it and your money in purchasing it. Tea bags tend to be more affordable, and they help meet the huge global demand for tea.

- **Accessibility:** For someone not from a country with a centuries-old tea culture, tea bags could be their first encounter with tea. Once they've tried it, they might then feel inspired to go further and explore the incredible flavors and aromas of unblended, loose-leaf tea.

WHAT TO LOOK FOR WHEN BUYING TEA BAGS

Sometimes convenience wins and you find yourself in need of tea bags. Here's how to spot a better-quality option.

1. **Shape:** Unlike the traditional flat bag, pyramid-shaped bags give the leaves more room to unfurl as they brew.

2. **Contents:** Companies such as Twinings, Tealyra, and Harney & Sons now offer bags containing loose-leaf or long-leaf tea, not fannings. These higher-quality bags are often called *tea sachets*.

3. **No additives:** Check the package to make sure the tea bags are free of sweeteners, artificial flavors or coloring, and other additives, which will impair the tea's flavor.

POPULAR TEA BLENDS

Tea bags are typically made from blends, which combine teas from several regions—some commercial blends can feature up to thirty different varieties! Although this means you'll miss out on the unique terroir of a pure, single-origin tea, blended teas also help achieve a more consistent taste. Here are some well-known black tea blends.

English breakfast

Strong. Robust. Full-bodied. You'll often hear these terms describing English breakfast tea, which features a mix of black teas from India, Kenya, and especially Sri Lanka. This blend's high level of tannins goes well with the milk and sugar often added to the tea.

Irish breakfast

Ireland is one of the top tea-drinking countries in the world—consuming nearly five pounds of tea per person a year—so it's little surprise that they have their own breakfast blend, in which malty Assam teas play a starring role.

Earl Grey

This classic British blend features black tea flavored with the oil of bergamot, an aromatic citrus fruit common in the Mediterranean.

HOW TO STORE TEA

The very things that define tea—such as the ease with which it absorbs other aromas, making teas such as Jasmine Pearls possible—also put it at risk of decay if it isn't stored properly. Follow these guidelines when storing your tea.

- **Keep it cool.** Cooler temperatures help tea stay fresh for longer periods, so avoid storing it near heat sources, such as a stove or oven.

- **Keep it dark.** Tea can also be damaged by light, so store it in opaque containers, preferably in a dark cabinet or drawer.

- **Keep it dry.** Moisture and humidity can both negatively affect tea (even leading to mold), so keep your tea away from steamy bathrooms or damp basements.

- **Keep it sealed.** Airtight containers—even if they're not perfectly air-free—help slow the oxidation process, which continues even after tea leaves have been dried, and prevent other odors from affecting your tea. Store your tea far from strong aromas; for instance, the spice cabinet is off-limits.

A NOTE ABOUT WATER QUALITY

"Water is the mother of tea, the teapot is its father, and fire the teacher."

—CHINESE PROVERB

There's a reason the Chinese call water "the mother of tea"—a cup of tea is around 98 percent water, so the quality of your H_2O is as important as the quality of the leaves. For great-tasting tea, follow these tips.

- Go neutral: The ideal water for brewing tea has a neutral pH of 7, meaning it's neither acidic nor basic. Evaluate your water's pH with testing strips, which can be ordered online and often cost less than $5.

- Avoid distilled and well water: Well water is usually high in minerals, which give tea a metallic taste, and the lack of natural minerals in distilled water will make tea taste flat.

- Use a filter: A filter reduces the chlorine and calcium often found in tap water—even a pitcher-style charcoal water filter can do the trick.

TEA ACCESSORIES

From fine-tuning the water temperature to measuring out the perfect amount of tea leaves, there's a lot to get right for a simple cup of tea. The following accessories are helpful for a tea lover to have on hand.

ESSENTIAL EQUIPMENT

- **Teapot and/or teacups:** If you're using small tea tasting cups—like those used in the traditional Chinese *gong fu* style of brewing (see page 96)—white or clear cups will help you appreciate the color of the liquor.

- **Tea infuser basket:** If your teapot doesn't have a built-in filter, you'll need an infuser. Although round tea ball infusers are common, their small size can prevent tea leaves from expanding in the water; tea infuser baskets give leaves more room to breathe and allow for more flavorful tea.

- **Tea filter bags:** Reusable tea bags and sachets are perfect for enjoying loose-leaf tea on the go; biodegradable filter bags are a great eco-friendly option.

- **Sweeteners:** Many loose-leaf teas, including green, white, and oolong, are often enjoyed straight, but if you take your tea milky and sweet, a sugar-and-creamer set is a must. Honey and agave nectar are alternative sweeteners, and a squeeze of fresh lemon gives your tea a healthy zing.

PREPARATION TOOLS

- **Thermometer:** The temperature of the water is one of the biggest variables to control when brewing tea, so a tea thermometer is crucial—some models even list the suggested temperatures for different types of tea on their cases.

- **Electric kettle:** Handy for heating up water in a hurry. Some models come with an internal thermometer and variable water temperature settings, saving you the need to invest in a separate thermometer.

- **Measuring spoon:** A helpful tool for every tea lover is a double-sided measuring spoon, with one end to measure the amount of loose-leaf tea for a cup and the other end for a full pot of tea. The next step up from a measuring spoon is a digital kitchen scale, which offers even greater precision.

- **Timer:** You could easily use your phone or kitchen timer to keep an eye on your infusion times, but a more elegant option is a sand timer. Some timers even come with three hourglass timers of different durations in one apparatus; this style is useful for anyone who regularly brews different types of tea.

- **Matcha tea whisk:** A more specialized accessory to have on hand is a bamboo whisk called the *chasen* in Japanese, which is used to stir matcha green tea powder with hot water to aerate the tea and give the beverage its signature creamy texture. (See page 99 for more on the matcha tea ceremony.)

FOR STORAGE

- **Tea canisters:** Store loose-leaf tea in airtight canisters made of ceramic or tin. Avoid glass containers, unless you're storing them in a dark place.

- **Tea chest:** Often made from wood with a glass lid, tea chests feature different compartments for organizing and storing tea bags; some models have a drawer for teaspoons or other small tea accessories.

TYPES OF TEAPOTS AND HOW TO USE THEM

"We had a kettle; we let it leak:
Our not repairing made it worse.
We haven't had any tea for a week . . .
The bottom is out of the Universe."

—RUDYARD KIPLING, "NATURAL THEOLOGY"

The world's first teapots most likely evolved from ancient Chinese wine ewers, which featured a spout and handle. Today, teapots come in all shapes and sizes. In the countries where tea originated, teapots also tend to be much smaller than Western-style tea ware. Here are four traditional vessels from across the globe—and why they're worth trying out.

WESTERN-STYLE TEAPOT

When it comes to teapots in the West, many resemble the rounded design of the quintessential British teapot, the Brown Betty, which is large enough to brew several cups of tea at a time. Like Chinese *yixing* teapots (see page 51), Brown Betty teapots are made from red clay, but whereas *yixing* teapots are left unglazed, the Brown Betty is treated with a manganese glaze that gives the teapot its distinctive dark color (and its name). Queen Victoria was said to have been a fan of the Brown Betty, which no doubt helped popularize it across England.

Best for: Black teas such as Assam, Darjeeling, and Ceylon

How to use it: As we'll talk more about in the next entry, a good rule of thumb for brewing tea Western-style in a larger teapot is one teaspoon of loose tea leaves per cup of water plus an additional teaspoon "for the pot"; or use one tea bag per cup of water.

GAIWAN

This traditional Chinese tea vessel has an impressive lineage, dating back to the Ming dynasty (1368–1644). *Gaiwan* literally translates as "lidded bowl," and it is comprised of three parts—a lid, a bowl, and a saucer. It's said that the lid represents the sky, the saucer the earth, and the bowl life.

A typical *gaiwan* is made from glazed porcelain, which means that—unlike with the *yixing* teapots we'll talk about below—you can prepare different kinds of tea in a single *gaiwan* and not have to worry about the taste being affected. The mouth of a *gaiwan*'s bowl is also wider than the opening on other teapots. This gives you a better view of the tea as it steeps, letting you watch the leaves swirl and unfurl in the water, and the aroma is also stronger as a result.

Best for: Lighter tea types such as white, green, and yellow teas

How to use it: Pour water over the leaves, using the appropriate water temperature and steeping time for the tea you've chosen (see page 61 for steeping times and temperatures), and then place the lid on the *gaiwan*. To decant the tea, place your index finger on the top of the lid, with your thumb and middle finger holding the rim of the bowl. Pour the tea into a sharing pitcher or directly into tasting cups.

YIXING

This iconic clay teapot gets its name from the Chinese city where a specific purple-red clay known as *zisha* is found; this material has been used to make Chinese pottery since the tenth century.

Because the unglazed clay is porous, it actually begins to absorb the flavors and aromas of tea over time—so much so that eventually the pot itself begins to contribute to the brew of the tea, giving it a rounder flavor. This means it's best to brew only one type of tea in a dedicated *yixing*, so as to avoid "cross-brewing" and mixing flavors.

Best for: Darker tea types such as oolong, black, and dark teas

How to use it: Start by pouring hot water over the teapot—this will require having a tea draining tray or tea boat under the pot, to collect the run-off water. Clay is amazing at retaining heat and keeping tea hot, and this step serves to warm up the pot before brewing.

Next, after placing the leaves in the teapot, do a quick tea rinse (also known as a tea wash) by adding fresh hot water to the pot, which helps the leaves "wake up" and gets rid of any tea dust or broken leaves. Think of the tea rinse as a "mini-infusion." But instead of waiting for the tea to steep, immediately pour the rinse into a pitcher that's known in Chinese as *gong dao bei*—the "fairness cup" or "fairness pitcher" that ensures everyone's tea has been evenly brewed.

Again, pour the rinse out over the teapot, as each wash helps develop the beautiful patina that *yixing* pots are known for. At last, you're ready for your first infusion and your first taste of this storied method of steeping tea. Infuse the rinsed leaves in the pot according to the recommended steep time and temperature.

KYUSU

This traditional Japanese teapot can be immediately recognized by its distinctive shape—namely, the tapered, hollow handle attached to its side. Like *gaiwan* and *yixing* teapots, it's much smaller than its Western counterparts, making it ideal for quick infusions and multiple servings.

Although *kyusu* teapots come in all manner of colors and styles, the classic version is made from iron-rich red clay. The most sought-after models hail from the historic Japanese pottery town of Tokoname. Many *kyusu* teapots also feature a built-in ceramic filter, though some are fitted with stainless-steel mesh strainers.

Best for: Japanese green teas, specifically nonpowdered teas such as *sencha*

How to use it: A good *kyusu* can be comfortably held in one hand, with your thumb placed over the lid, and poured with a simple twist of the wrist. In lieu of a fairness pitcher, this method employs a different technique when serving multiple cups of tea: alternate among cups as you pour, since the infusion is still taking place even as you're pouring. Also be sure to completely decant the teapot, ensuring that no water is left with the leaves. In Japan, the very last bit is known as the as the "golden drop," and it is full of the tea's aroma, taste, and umami. Repeat and enjoy!

CARE AND CLEANING OF TEAPOTS

- **Unglazed clay teapots:** Avoid detergent or stain removers such as vinegar, which could be absorbed by the unglazed clay and impart unpleasant flavor to your next brew. To wash a *yixing* teapot, remove the used tea leaves and rinse the pot with hot water; be sure to let it dry with its lid off, to prevent mold from growing.

- **Glazed teapots:** Use mild dish soap with porcelain or other glazed teapots. Vinegar and baking soda can also help remove stains and tannin buildup.

TEA PETS

Take a look at a traditional *gong fu* tea setup, and you'll no doubt spy a small clay figurine perched in a corner of the tea tray. This is a tea pet.

A brief history: Tea pets date to the Yuan dynasty in China (1206–1368), when artisans began to mold small animals or mythical creatures from the same *zisha* clay they used to make *yixing* teapots.

How to "feed" your pet: Because clay tea pets are left unglazed, their porous surfaces can develop the same rich patina as *yixing* teapots. To feed and "nourish" your tea pet, regularly pour liquid over it while preparing tea *gong fu* style—not only the hot water you use to warm up the teapot, but also the tea rinse and any leftover steeped tea. Like *yixing* teapots, tea pets will gradually take on the aroma and color of tea.

Why have a tea pet? Why not! Tea pets add a touch of beauty and decoration to your tea tray, and some believe certain tea pets even play a more symbolic role, inviting blessings and good luck.

Popular designs: Many tea pets are animals from the Chinese zodiac, such as the ox, which is a symbol of strength, and the pig, representing wealth and good luck. Money frogs are used to invite prosperity, while the laughing Buddha represents contentment.

HOW TO PREPARE TEA

*"You can never get a cup of tea large enough
or a book long enough to suit me."*

—C. S. LEWIS

From terroir to tannins, we've covered many things that wine and tea have in common—but there's also a big difference between them. Though both require in-depth knowledge and a discerning palate, all you really need to know to prepare a glass of wine is how to open the bottle.

With tea, however, the process is more hands-on and dynamic. We have to pair our knowledge of tea with the practical skills of how to prepare it, too. When it comes to tea making, three main variables are in our control:

1. Water temperature

2. Steeping time

3. Water-to-leaf ratio

The last variable lies at the heart of two very different approaches to brewing tea.

TEA PREPARATION: EAST VS. WEST

You may be familiar with the Japanese tea ceremony, but how about the Chinese tea-drinking tradition known as *gong fu cha*? This method is also known as kung fu, and you'll be forgiven if the first thing that just came to mind was a Bruce Lee action scene. But the phrase *kung fu* itself doesn't actually refer to the Chinese martial arts. Kung fu—or as it's written in Pinyin, *gong fu*—translates as "skill," especially one that has taken time and effort to master. *Gong fu cha* thus means "preparing tea with great effort and skill."

A traditional *gong fu* brewing session will feature either a porcelain *gaiwan* or an unglazed clay teapot, and yet it's important to know that *gong fu* is about so much more than just the vessels and tools used to prepare the tea. In Western tea traditions, the tendency is to brew a small amount of tea in a large teapot; what's more, the leaves are typically steeped only once. *Gong fu* brewing turns this method on its head, using a greater amount of tea leaves with a smaller amount of water. This setup allows for multiple short infusions, meaning you can brew several servings of liquor from a single portion of tea leaves before the leaves must be discarded.

Not only does the *gong fu* method result in a richer, more concentrated taste, but it also allows you to enjoy the nuances of the tea as it gradually evolves from one infusion to the next—a quality oolong or *pu-erh* tea can be infused up to ten times! After the first infusion, you'll want to gradually increase your steeping time, until you sense that the leaves have lost their flavor and are no longer good for additional infusions.

ONE POT OF HOT TEA

Before tea leaves even reach the pot, the distinction between Western and *gong fu*–style brewing methods is immediately evident in their tea ware. Whereas a classic English teapot may hold around 6 to 8 cups of water, a Chinese tea vessel such as a *gaiwan* or *yixing* teapot may hold just 6 to 8 *ounces*, if not less.

The Western approach to brewing follows a water-to-leaf ratio of one teaspoon of tea leaves per cup of water—plus "one for the pot," if you follow the old British adage. The *gong fu* method calls for leaves measured by general volume—the idea is to fill the tea vessel anywhere from a third to halfway full, depending on the size of the dry leaves.

Both approaches advise using spring or filtered water, and you'll also want to warm your tea vessel with hot water before brewing, no matter its size. The last remaining variable is how long you let the tea leaves steep, whether for a matter of seconds (*gong fu*) or minutes (Western). For recommended infusion times and water temperatures, see the chart on page 61.

ONE CUP OF HOT TEA

While the *gong fu* style gives tea a lovely, full flavor, there are other times that call for brewing a simple cuppa for one. In those moments, the Western-style ratio stays the same: either one tea bag or a teaspoon of loose tea leaves to one cup of water. Don't forget to remove the bag after it's done steeping.

> Tip: Definitely don't squeeze your tea bag when it's finished steeping. This will only release unwanted extra tannins.

HOT-BREWED ICED TEA

Since the first known recipe for iced tea was published in 1879, in a community cookbook called *Housekeeping in Old Virginia*, the traditional method for brewing iced tea hasn't changed much.

Use either one tea bag or one teaspoon of loose-leaf tea for every cup of water. Brew the tea just as you would a pot of hot tea; for sweetened iced tea, add sugar (the amount will depend on just how Southern-sweet you like your tea). Finally, let the tea cool in the refrigerator for at least four hours before serving it over ice—perhaps with a twist of lemon or mint.

COLD-BREWED ICED TEA

If you've ever been turned off by the bitter edge to iced tea—or if you've gotten caffeine jitters after one too many cups of the stuff—cold-brewing your iced tea is the way to go. The water-to-leaf ratio is a little higher than for normal hot-brewed tea; use 1½ teaspoons of leaves, or 1½ tea bags, per cup of water. The water can be anywhere from cold to room temperature.

All that's left to do is let the tea steep in the refrigerator for 8 to 10 hours. Cold-brewing tea is a slow infusion process that's nearly impossible to oversteep. Tannins and caffeine both need heat to be extracted from tea leaves, so by cold-brewing you'll get less astringency *and* less caffeine—in fact, a cup of cold-brewed iced tea often has less than half the caffeine of a cup of hot-brewed tea.

RECOMMENDED STEEP TIMES AND WATER TEMPERATURES

To get your tea infusions right, follow this easy guideline: the more oxidized a tea is, the higher the temperature you can brew it with. Also keep in mind that these suggested steep times apply to Western-style brewing; *gong fu* infusions will generally be much shorter.

TEA FAMILY	BREWING TIMES & TEMPERATURES
White tea	3–4 minutes 160°F–180°F (71°C–82°C)
Green tea	1–2 minutes 160°F–180°F (71°C–82°C)
Yellow tea	2–3 minutes 160°F–175°F (71°C–79°C)
Oolong tea	2–5 minutes 180°F–200°F (82°C–93°C)
Black tea	3–5 minutes 190°F–212°F (88°C–100°C)
Dark tea	2–5 minutes 200°F–212°F (93°C–100°C)

TEA FAMILIES & COMMON VARIETIES

BLACK TEA

When someone from the West pictures a cup of tea, chances are they're envisioning a sweet, milky mug of black tea. In fact, 90 percent of tea sold in Western markets today is black tea. Let's dive into the history behind this ubiquitous brew. (Throughout this chapter, keep an eye out for the Chinese names of some tea varieties, which we've shared to honor tea's ancient roots.)

HISTORY OF BLACK TEA

The tea, the myth, the legend: Ever since those first fateful leaves drifted towards Emperor Shen Nung and transformed his water into tea, the world of tea has been filled with myths—and so does the story of black tea begin with such a tale. They say that around the year 1590, in the Chinese province of Fujian, a passing army arrived in the Wuyi Mountains. They sought shelter at a tea factory, where tea leaves had been laid out in the sun to wither. But the soldiers' arrival delayed the tea farmers in their work and the leaves were left out far longer than normal, which caused them to darken and oxidize. The next day, hoping to speed up the drying process, the farmers built a fire out of pinewood and proceeded to smoke-dry the leaves. The resulting smoky tea was Lapsang souchong, which is now considered one of the original black teas.

East meets West: The timing of this serendipitous discovery of black tea in China happened to coincide with the Western world's discovery of tea. The Dutch first brought tea back from China to Europe in 1606, and black tea's swift rise in popularity among European markets no doubt had as much to do with its long shelf life as with its bold flavor; being much more processed than green tea, black tea was better suited for surviving those lengthy ocean journeys.

Tea espionage: Black tea became so popular in England that by the nineteenth century, the British were no longer content relying on China, who at that point was still the world's sole producer of tea. The British demand for tea was even the impetus behind both Opium Wars, which devastated the Chinese economy (see page 17). In 1823, a second variety of the tea plant known as *Camellia sinensis var. assamica* was discovered, indigenous to the Assam region of India. By 1848, a Mandarin-speaking Scottish botanist named Robert Fortune smuggled tea plants and valuable notes for growing and processing tea from China to Assam—which is now the largest tea-growing region in the world.

CHARACTERISTICS OF BLACK TEA

- **Popular growing countries:** China, India, Kenya, Sri Lanka, Turkey, Indonesia, Argentina

- **Flavor profiles:** A range of strong flavors, from fruity and floral to malty, spicy, and smoky

- **Brewing tips:** Generally brewed at a higher temperature than green tea (200°F–212°F, or 93°C–100°C) and for longer, typically 3–5 minutes

- **Appearance of dry leaves:** Dark brown; may have some golden leaves, depending on the number of buds or tips present

- **Color(s) of the liquor:** Coppery red and amber to brown

POPULAR BLACK TEA VARIETIES

Lapsang Souchong (*Zhen Shan Xiao Chung*)

China's first black tea continues to be one of its most famous, and just as in its origin legend, Lapsang souchong is still produced by drying the leaves over pinewood fires, which gives the tea its signature smoky profile. We can learn a lot about this tea from its name alone: *souchong* refers to the fourth and fifth leaves from each stem on a tea plant. Though not as prized as the buds or first two leaves, souchong leaves are larger and can withstand the smoke-drying process.

Keemun (Qi Men Hong Cha)

Keemun is a newer Chinese black tea, from Qimen county in Anhui Province in eastern China (Keemun is the colonial spelling of Qimen). Its origin story dates to 1875, when a civil servant from Anhui traveled to Fujian Province to learn how to process black tea. He then took those techniques home and found the resulting tea was a hit—especially with the British, who used Keemun as one of the first base teas in their English breakfast blend. Because the leaves are both withered and oxidized more slowly than other varieties of black tea, Keemun has a rich, nuanced flavor profile, marked by a sweet, floral aroma and notes of cocoa and fruit.

Assam

Unblended black teas are usually named after the region where they're grown, and this prominent variety hails from the lush Brahmaputra Valley in eastern India—home to the second, large-leafed variety of the tea plant, *Camellia sinensis var. assamica*. Unlike Darjeeling tea, which is grown at elevations of up to

7,000 feet, Assam is grown in low-lying floodplains at sea level. Both the region's humid, tropical climate and its nutrient-rich clay soil help give this tea its characteristic malty, full-bodied flavor.

Darjeeling

Tucked away in the foothills of the Himalayas, the region of Darjeeling in northeast India produces one of the world's finest black teas. Unlike the majority of Indian teas, Darjeeling is made from the small-leaf Chinese variety of *Camellia sinensis*, and its distinctive muscatel flavor has led to its reputation as "the Champagne of teas." Although there can be up to five harvests—or flushes—a year, first- and second-flush Darjeelings are the most sought-after, as are those from single tea estates. Because it is less oxidized than other black tea varieties, Darjeeling should be brewed at slightly lower temperatures, around 180°F–195°F (82°C–90°C).

Ceylon

For half a century, coffee was one of the principal crops of Sri Lanka (formerly known as Ceylon)—until a devastating blight wiped out the island's plantations in the second half of the 1800s. In 1890, things began to turn around, thanks to a name you might recognize: Thomas Lipton. The Scottish tea merchant bought 3,000 acres of land and soon created global demand for Ceylon tea, his slogan promising a product that was "direct from the tea garden to the tea pot." Today's Ceylon teas vary in quality and character according to the altitude where they're grown, from the strong, dark profile of low-grown teas to the lighter, more delicate high-grown varieties.

Kenyan

Commercial tea production in Kenya didn't begin until 1924, when the country was under British colonial rule. Despite its late start, Kenya is now the largest tea producer in Africa, the third largest producer in the world—outdone only by China and India—and one of the world's top tea exporters. Kenyan black tea is known for being robust and full-bodied, and it's frequently used in blends such as English breakfast. Today, over 60 percent of Kenyan tea is grown by small-scale tea farmers.

GRADES OF BLACK TEA

SFTGFOP—if you've perused a selection of loose-leaf black teas, chances are you've seen some combination of these letters next to the name of a tea. No matter how jumbled they might seem, the letters aren't random; instead, they're part of a grading system used to classify black teas from places such as India, Sri Lanka, Kenya, and other countries whose tea production was influenced by British colonial rule. (Note: In China, tea leaves are given a grade based on appearance; 1 is the highest, and 7, or sometimes 9, is the lowest.)

Grades are based on the size and visual appearance of the tea leaf—whether the leaves are whole, broken, or crushed—and from which part of the leaf a tea is made. In general, the more letters you see next to a tea's name, the higher its quality. Common grading terms include the following.

GRADES OF WHOLE LEAVES

OP: Orange pekoe. This term denotes basic whole-leaf black tea—*not* the tea's flavor or color, despite some Western teas being marketed as such. Orange most likely refers to the royal House of Orange in the Netherlands. Pekoe is derived from the Chinese word *pak-ho*, which means "white down" and refers to the downy hairs on young, unopened tea buds.

FOP: Flowery orange pekoe. Includes some leaf buds, or tips. The more tips that are present in a tea, the higher its quality.

GFOP: Golden flowery orange pekoe. Golden refers to very young tea buds, which turn a golden color when they're oxidized.

SFTGFOP: Special finest tippy golden flowery orange pekoe. The highest grade of black tea. *Tippy* means the tea has a high concentration of those high-quality leaf buds, or tips.

GRADES OF BROKEN LEAVES

BOP: Broken orange pekoe. Broken leaves create a strong brew.

Fannings: One of the lowest grades of black tea, comprising small particles of tea leaves. Fannings are typically used in tea bags.

Dust: The smallest crushed particles of tea produced by the orthodox method. Also used for tea bags.

GREEN TEA

If Shen Nung first discovered tea in 2737 BCE and black tea wasn't produced until the seventeenth century, what tea was the world drinking for all those thousands of years in between? The answer is green tea, and it's still as prevalent today in China and Japan as black tea is in the West.

HISTORY OF GREEN TEA

The birthplace of tea: Green tea is the oldest of the six tea families, and in many ways, the history of green tea *is* the history of tea. In imperial China, each dynasty brought about a new development, in both the way tea was processed and the place it held in society. For instance, in the Ming dynasty (1368–1644) cakes and bricks of tea were prohibited by Emperor Hongwu, who came from the peasant class. In his own words, he felt that the labor-intensive process of making compressed tea "greatly strains the resources of the people." This led to the invention of loose-leaf tea, which in turn led to the teapot; whereas cake teas had been ground into a powder and whisked in tea bowls, the new method of steeping loose tea leaves inspired both *gaiwans* and *yixing* teapots. Today, 80 percent of the world's green tea is produced by China.

Zen and the art of tea: From China, tea gradually made its way to neighboring countries, all thanks to a singular evangelist: Buddhist monks. The qualities we still value tea for today—its ability to calm and relax our minds while also making us more alert—made it a welcome aid for long hours of meditation, a vital practice in Zen Buddhism. After monks from Japan and Korea traveled to China to study, they returned home with two important souvenirs—Zen scriptures and tea seeds. In ancient Korea, the worlds of tea and Buddhism were so closely linked that a statue of Buddha was often displayed in public tea houses, and green tea was a common offering to Buddha.

Tea warriors: Monks weren't the only proponents of tea in ancient Japan; so was the ruling samurai class taken with the physical and spiritual benefits of tea. Though it almost sounds like something out of a storybook, it is well documented that samurai would leave their swords outside before entering a tea house. And in the sixteenth century, Buddhist monk and tea master Sen no Rikyū created a small, low doorway for his tea house known as *nijiriguchi*, which is still used in Japanese tea houses today. The entrance required everyone—including the mighty samurai—to bow as they entered the tea house, as a sign of humility.

CHARACTERISTICS OF GREEN TEA

- **Popular growing countries:** China, Japan, Indonesia, Vietnam

- **Flavor profiles:** Pan-fired green teas can taste grassy, earthy, and toasted. Steamed green teas have sweeter, vegetal notes, often suggestive of seaweed.

- **Brewing tips:** Brewed at lower temperatures than black tea (around 160°F–180°F, or 71°C–82°C) and for less time, generally 1–2 minutes

- **Appearance of dry leaves:** The many processing styles for green tea result in a variety of shapes, from finely ground matcha to gunpowder, whose leaves are tightly rolled into small round pellets.

- **Color(s) of the liquor:** Pale olive or emerald green; straw yellow

POPULAR GREEN TEA VARIETIES

Matcha

In 1191, a Buddhist monk named Eisai brought the Chinese method of whipped, powdered tea back to Japan, where it became an essential component of the Japanese tea ceremony—as it still is today. To produce matcha, the tea plants are shade-grown for several weeks before harvest. As the leaves receive less sunlight than they would if grown in direct sun, chlorophyll levels shoot up, giving the tea a sweeter taste; ceremonial-grade matcha should thus be a vivid green. The leaves are then stone-ground into a fine powder, which makes matcha the only tea whose leaves are consumed directly (rather than infused). Finally, matcha is mixed with water using a traditional bamboo whisk called the *chasen*, which helps create the tea's iconic creamy texture.

Sencha

This variety is the most popular tea in Japan, comprising more than 80 percent of the tea produced in that country. It is known for its vegetal notes and mild astringency. Translated as "infused tea," *sencha* is distinct from matcha in a few important ways. Not only is it grown in full sunlight, but its leaves are left whole and rolled into a distinctive needle shape. One sought-after type is *shincha*, which means "new tea" and is made from the first *sencha* harvest of the year.

Kukicha

This Japanese green tea is part of a unique group: twig teas! *Kuki* literally means "twig" or "stem," and that's exactly what goes into *kukicha*: the stems and stalks of the tea plant. When quality green teas such as matcha are processed in Japan, the leaves are deveined and destemmed. Many years ago, resourceful farmers had the idea to make a tea out of these by-products of the more valuable leaves and buds, and as such, it was known as the "peasant's tea." The stems give the tea a sweet, nutty flavor—especially true of toasted *kukicha*—and it is also very low in caffeine.

Genmaicha

From verdant matcha powder to the twigs and stems of *kukicha*, Japanese green teas can often be recognized by the shape of their dry leaf. *Genmaicha* is another easily identified example, which features green tea leaves mixed with kernels of roasted, puffed rice—some of which pop while being roasted and give *genmaicha* its nickname, "popcorn tea." While many myths surround its origin, it most likely dates to the 1900s, when tea merchants tried to make their expensive green tea more affordable by adding rice to it. Despite its humble beginnings, *genmaicha* is now popular around the world.

Jasmine Dragon Pearls (Mo Li Long Zhu)

Although tea's ability to absorb aromas and flavors means it shouldn't be stored near a spice cabinet, it also makes a special category of tea possible: scented teas. Since the Ming dynasty, the Chinese have practiced scenting teas with fresh flowers, including rose, magnolia, and plum blossoms—but most famous of all is jasmine. High-grade Jasmine Pearl teas are created by layering budsets of green tea leaves with jasmine blossoms. The leaves absorb the flowers' sweet fragrance, and are then rolled into pearls. In *The Tea Enthusiast's Handbook*, tea experts Mary Lou Heiss and Robert Heiss suggest using 8 to 10 pearls with 6 ounces of water.

WHITE TEA

Black and green tea are perhaps the best-known teas in the world—and the most widely consumed. The next two families of tea we'll look at are the rarest, starting with white tea.

HISTORY OF WHITE TEA

A royal favorite: A few centuries after Lu Yu penned his defining tome (see page 37), another Chinese tea master wrote his own seminal text: Song dynasty emperor Huizong, who published *The Treatise on Tea* in 1107. Known as the "Tea Emperor," he is even said to have prepared his own tea—something that was highly unusual at the time. White tea was his favorite. As he described it in his treatise: "White tea is unique amongst all the tea under Heaven."

Monkey business: Rumor has it that in the birthplace of white tea—the Chinese province of Fujian—the region's steep, soaring mountains held wild tea trees not reachable by man. So how were those precious tea leaves to be harvested? Buddhist monks allegedly trained monkeys to scale the cliffs and pick leaves from the trees beyond the monks' reach. Though there's probably little truth to this legend, the phrase "monkey-picked" is still used today with some tea varieties, to suggest higher quality.

Provenance matters: Although India, Sri Lanka, and even Malawi have started to produce white teas, the original source of this tea family is important. Only those white teas grown in Fujian are considered authentic—just as true Champagne comes only from the Champagne region of France and only dark teas from Yunnan Province in China can be called *pu-erh*.

CHARACTERISTICS OF WHITE TEA

- **Popular growing countries:** China, India, Sri Lanka

- **Flavor profiles:** Light oxidation results in a soft, smooth taste, often with sweet or floral notes.

- **Brewing tips:** Like green tea, white tea is brewed at milder temperatures (160°F–180°F, or 71°C–82°C) for around 2–3 minutes, although the leaves are somewhat forgiving and can withstand longer steeping times.

- **Appearance of dry leaves:** Look for lots of buds, especially with Silver Needle, and for the white downy hairs that give this class of tea its name.

- **Color(s) of the liquor:** Pale yellow, light honey

POPULAR WHITE TEA VARIETIES

Silver Needle (*Bai Hao Yin Zhen*)

Every spring, in the misty mountains of Fujian Province, the highest grade of white tea is made. The harvest for Silver Needle begins with the plucking of only the youngest, unopened buds, before they've had a chance to unfurl. The buds are picked by hand so that they aren't damaged, especially the fine downy hair covering each bud. The result is a rare and highly prized tea, known for its delicate, floral aroma and smooth, sweet flavor profile.

White Peony (*Bai Mu Dan*)

Given that Silver Needle uses only the delicate bud of the tea plant, it commands a high price. In the 1920s, a more affordable variety of white tea was created, utilizing the buds and the first two leaves of the tea plant: White Peony, named for how the leaves resemble a peony as they unfurl in hot water. White Peony is the second highest grade of white tea produced in China today, offering a full body with fruity, nutty notes.

YELLOW TEA

Just 1 percent of tea is considered true yellow tea, so it's little surprise that many people haven't heard of this rare family and that others assume it's no different from green tea. Learning more about yellow tea is a surefire way to level up from tea lover to tea connoisseur.

HISTORY OF YELLOW TEA

The princess and the tea: Yellow tea has a long and storied past in China, dating back to the T'ang dynasty. In the seventh century, T'ang princess Wencheng was married to Tibetan king Songstan Gambo. Tucked away in her trousseau was tea, which she carried with her to Tibet. It's said that the tea was *Jun Shan Yin Zhen*, one of the rarest varieties of yellow tea. This introduced the Tibetans to tea, which then led to the development of the ancient Tea Horse Road—helping Tibetans supplement their meat-heavy diet with tea, while the Chinese received much-needed war horses.

Tea tributes: Long before British taxes incited the Boston Tea Party in the American colonies, the imperial court of China had been demanding a tea tax in the form of tea tributes—known as *gong cha* in Chinese. As early as the fifth century, tea farmers across the country were required to give their finest teas to the emperor, and certain varieties were even produced specifically as tribute teas. Yellow tea became one such tea, but not only because of its high quality; its color also held deep significance. Yellow was the official color of the imperial court—the emperor wore yellow robes, yellow flags were flown on the emperor's tours, and only the homes of the royal family could be fitted with yellow roof tiles. For many years, yellow tea was reserved exclusively for the emperor, thus making it as prized and rare then as it is today.

The chairman's brew: Yellow tea wasn't just the preferred class of tea for ancient emperors and princesses; in more recent history, the story goes that Mao Zedong also declared yellow tea his favorite, specifically the *Jun Shan Yin Zhen* variety cultivated on Junshan Island in Hunan Province. Given that the chairman was from that province, there is some weight to this claim.

CHARACTERISTICS OF YELLOW TEA

- Popular growing countries: China

- Flavor profiles: The slight fermentation the leaves undergo during processing gives yellow tea a more mellow taste, without the grassy notes of green tea.

- **Brewing tips:** Yellow tea is brewed at similar temperatures to green tea (around 160°F–175°F, or 71°C–79°C) and steeped for 2–3 minutes.

- **Appearance of dry leaves:** Long, yellowish buds or budsets shaped like needles or spears

- **Color(s) of the liquor:** Straw-yellow, golden

POPULAR YELLOW TEA VARIETY

Mount Jun Silver Needle (*Jun Shan Yin Zhen*)

This variety of yellow tea is the rarest tea made in China, for a number of reasons. Junshan Island is just one square kilometer in area, so the growing region is extremely small. The processing is also lengthy and labor-intensive, requiring the work of expert tea masters who today are few and far between. *Jun Shan Yin Zhen* has even been described as the "modern tribute tea" because the sweet, bud-only variety is often reserved for government officials and foreign diplomats—just as it was during the Qing dynasty.

OOLONG TEA

Oolong tea is a world unto itself. Different levels of oxidation combined with the diverse terroirs of the main growing regions have led to an array of oolong styles, shapes, and flavors.

HISTORY OF OOLONG TEA

The birthplace of oolong: The Chinese province of Fujian was the birthplace of three distinct families of tea—white, black (especially Lapsang souchong), and oolong, which was developed by monks after cake teas were prohibited in the Ming dynasty. During the eighteenth and nineteenth centuries, it was Fujianese emigrants who carried tea plants with them from mainland China to Taiwan and helped establish the island's now-thriving tea culture.

Feeling the blues: The family of oolong tea is known in Chinese as *qing cha*, which means "blue tea." Every other tea was named for the color of its liquor; oolong is named for the color of its dry leaves, which can have a blue or teal sheen. The dry leaves can also give you an idea of how oxidized the tea is, whether they're closer in hue to green (less oxidized) or black (more oxidized).

Oolong crash course: Finding your way in the world of oolong teas for the first time can be an overwhelming endeavor, especially as the names of varieties often vary and are not as recognizable as, say, an Assam or Ceylon. Here are the four main types of oolong organized by growing region:

1. **Anxi:** In the south of Fujian, Anxi County is famous for oolong production, creating teas that are lightly oxidized and often rolled into balls.

2. **Wuyi:** The darkest style of oolong is produced in the Wuyi mountains of north Fujian, where the landscape's limestone cliffs and rocky soil play a key role in giving the tea rich, earthy notes and minerality—so much so that these teas are also known as rock oolongs or cliff tea.

3. **Dancong:** This category is also known as Phoenix oolong because it is grown on Phoenix Mountain in Guangdong Province. *Dancong* means "single bush"; the tea is often harvested from single old tea trees. Even more remarkably, Dancong oolongs mimic the aromas of different fruits and flowers, and so each tea is named after its distinct fragrance. *Mi Lan Xiang*, or "honey orchid," is a

popular variety; others include jasmine, almond, and cinnamon.

4. **Taiwan:** No chapter on oolong tea would be complete without Taiwan, where oolong comprises over 90 percent of the island's total tea production. As Taiwan was formerly known as Formosa (Portuguese for "beautiful"), another name for this category is Formosa oolongs.

CHARACTERISTICS OF OOLONG TEA

- **Popular growing countries:** China, Taiwan, Vietnam

- **Flavor profiles:** Oolong teas can range in taste from sweet and floral to nutty and toasted.

- **Brewing tips:** Make the most of oolong's complex flavors with multiple infusions (at least 3–5), at temperatures of 180°F–200°F (82°C–93°C).

- **Appearance of dry leaves:** Oolong leaves are typically either rolled into a ball or left long and twisted in what's known as "strip style."

- **Color(s) of the liquor:** Varies from light green and golden to dark amber and brown

POPULAR OOLONG TEA VARIETIES

Dong Ding Oolong

Also known as Tung Ting, this renowned Taiwanese oolong dates to the mid-nineteenth century, when a scholar from Nantou County in central Taiwan traveled to Fujian for his civil service exam. Upon returning home from China, he brought thirty-six tea seedlings with him and planted them on a mountain named Dong Ding, which means "frozen summit" or "icy peak." Taiwan's high-mountain oolongs are prized for their complex flavors, and Dong Ding is one of the most popular oolong teas today, known for its lighter oxidation, tightly rolled ball shape, and sweet, buttery notes.

Oriental Beauty (*Dong Fang Mei Ren*)

For most teas, oxidation doesn't begin until after the leaves are plucked, but this notable oolong from northern Taiwan gets an early start—thanks to a tiny insect known as the tea jassid, or leafhopper. While the leaves are still growing, they're bitten by jassids and other insects. In defense, the plant releases an aromatic compound known as terpene. This makes the leaves markedly sweeter and initiates early oxidation, resulting in a highly oxidized tea. From its unique processing to its unmistakable fruity fragrance, Oriental Beauty is one of the most sought-after oolongs in the world.

Iron Goddess of Mercy (*Tie Guan Yin*)

The premium Anxi oolong *Tie Guan Yin*, or Iron Goddess of Mercy, is the most famous variety of all oolong teas. It can be identified by its flowery aroma and distinctive half-ball shape. A unique take on this variety is ginseng oolong, which encloses the balled tea leaves in a shell of compressed ginseng powder and gives the tea a refreshing, piquant taste. Brewing tip: Use a glass teapot or *gaiwan* so you can watch the pellets dissolve and the leaves gradually unfurl in hot water.

DARK TEA

Known as *hei cha* in Chinese, dark tea is the only class of tea that is fully fermented. Although you may associate fermentation with alcoholic drinks such as beer and wine, dark teas also experience the effects of natural bacteria and microbes. Thus, these teas are the only family that gets better with age, whereas other teas just get old.

HISTORY OF DARK TEA

Tea Horse Road: Fermented teas got their start more than a thousand years ago, when trade routes were developed between Tibet and Yunnan Province in southern China. In preparation for the long journey ahead, tea was packed into bricks or flat, round cakes known as *bing cha*. These were then wrapped in bamboo and placed on horses, mules, or porters, who could carry up to two hundred pounds of tea. As the caravans made their way north along winding mountain trails, all those bricks of tea were exposed to the elements: to humidity, heat from the sun, and moisture from rain and snow. The entire journey contributed to the changing flavors of the tea, leading to a natural fermentation that became highly sought-after. Even Qing dynasty emperor Fu Yi is said to have remarked, "Drinking *pu-erh* tea is like being a member of the royal family."

The *pu-erh* bubble: Today one type of dark tea still undergoes natural fermentation; these raw dark teas are known in Chinese as *sheng*. But in the 1970s, a process for artificial fermentation was developed, resulting in the second type of dark tea known as *shu* (also referred to as cooked or ripe). As the aging process for *pu-erh* was sped up, thanks to a special method of wet-piling the leaves known as *wo dui*, its popularity grew. During the 1990s and 2000s, the price for *pu-erh* shot to unprecedented heights; in 2005, 500 grams of one vintage *pu-erh* sold for the modest sum of $150,000. But this also led to an influx of counterfeit tea and false advertising, and in 2007, the *pu-erh* bubble finally burst over the course of just a few days. To read more about this wild time in the world of tea, check out Lisa See's novel *The Tea Girl of Hummingbird Lane*.

The drinkable antique: Despite its recent state of affairs, *pu-erh* is still cherished by tea lovers; it's even known as a "drinkable antique," because it only grows more complex and flavorful with time. Some connoisseurs have gone so far as to take their tea cake on a pilgrimage to its place of origin.

CHARACTERISTICS OF DARK TEA

- **Popular growing countries:** China, Japan, Vietnam, Myanmar

- **Flavor profiles:** Dark teas vary greatly due to their different ages and aging methods. Raw *pu-erh* tends to offer vegetal, more bitter notes, whereas ripe *pu-erh* has a smoother, woodsy flavor.

- **Brewing tips:** Dark tea is best brewed *gong fu* style, in a *gaiwan* or *yixing* teapot. *Sheng pu-erh* teas should be brewed at temperatures around 200°F (93°C); *shu pu-erh* teas are more robust and can be brewed with boiling water.

- **Appearance of dry leaves:** Dark teas come in loose-leaf form or compressed into round cakes or bricks.

- **Color(s) of the liquor:** Bright yellow (*sheng pu-erh*) to deep reddish-brown (*shu pu-erh*)

POPULAR DARK TEA VARIETIES

Pu-erh

Pu-erh is as complex a world to explore as oolong. If you're just getting started with this fascinating variety, many companies sell sample sizes, which allow you to discover what styles you're drawn to without needing to invest in a full-sized tea cake. Like Champagne, true *pu-erh* is grown only in Yunnan Province—considered the birthplace of tea—and it must be made from the large-leaf *Camellia sinensis var. assamica* plant. If both of those conditions are met, you'll find a certificate embedded in your tea cake. This is called the *nei fei* and lists the factory and year of production, guaranteeing your *pu-erh* is the real deal.

Liu An

Pu-erh is by far the most recognized dark tea, especially in the West, so take your tea game to the next level by exploring lesser-known dark tea varieties, such as the rare *Liu An* basket tea, from Anhui Province. Its very name hints at the unique way the tea is made; before being bake-dried, the processed tea is packaged into small, hand-woven bamboo baskets that are lined with bamboo leaves.

Liu Bao

Liu Bao originated in the province of Guangxi, where it was traditionally smoke-dried over pinewood fires and aged in large bamboo baskets. Both of these processing steps help give *Liu Bao* its distinctive earthiness, with notes of camphor and betel nut.

A NOTE ABOUT TISANES AND HERBAL TEAS

The six families of tea discussed on pages 64–89 are all considered true teas because they are made from the leaves of the *Camellia sinensis* plant. This means that everything else, from rooibos in South Africa to yerba mate in South America, isn't technically tea, but rather an herbal infusion—also called a *tisane*.

Many tisanes are caffeine free and offer an array of health benefits, too. Peppermint aids digestion, chamomile and valerian root can help treat insomnia, and rose hips contain far more vitamin C than oranges! To make your own, simply place a few of the following ingredients in your mug, add boiling water, and steep for several minutes.

- Flowers: Chamomile, hibiscus, rose hips
- Fruits: Apple, elderberry, raspberry
- Herbs: Lemon verbena, mint, rosemary
- Roots: Ginger, echinacea, turmeric
- Spices: Cardamom, cinnamon, clove

TEA TRADITIONS ACROSS THE WORLD

CHINA'S *GONG FU CHA*

"A day without tea is a day without joy."

—CHINESE PROVERB

Gong fu cha is a traditional Chinese method of brewing tea with a high ratio of leaves to water, which allows for multiple short infusions. It's often thought of today as a national custom, but in fact the practice has deep regional roots in southern China, specifically the coastal provinces of Fujian and Guangdong—some folks even refer to the city of Chaozhou as the "capital of *gong fu* tea." Although *gong fu cha* most likely originated in the eighteenth century, only in recent decades has it been elevated into a widespread tea tradition across China and Taiwan.

A key element of *gong fu* brewing is the equipment used for preparing the tea. Historically there were "four treasures" of *gong fu cha*: a charcoal stove, a kettle, a small *yixing* clay teapot, and porcelain tasting cups. Other accessories include a *gong dao bei*, known as a fairness cup or fairness pitcher; aroma cups for perceiving the scents of the liquor before drinking; and a tea draining tray, as well as a bamboo tea scoop and tongs for handling the tea leaves.

A typical *gong fu* brewing session will use darker types of tea such as oolong and *pu-erh*, and as we explored earlier (see page 52), there are three key steps to preparing tea *gong fu* style—warming up the teapot and cups with hot water over a tea draining tray, "waking up" the leaves with a tea rinse, and finally infusing the tea for short periods of time. People being served tea *gong fu* style participate in the experience by utilizing the aroma and tasting cups to appreciate the tea's fragrance and flavor. Rather than pouring tea into individual teacups one at a time, which will result in servings of different strengths, the tea may be poured into a fairness pitcher before being divided among individual teacups, ensuring an even brew for all. (Note: if you're using aroma cups, pour the tea into these first, before transferring the liquid to teacups for tasting.) Although *gong fu cha* is often referred to today as a ceremony—likening it to the centuries-old Japanese tea ceremony (see page 99)—it is essentially a style of preparing tea with great skill, attention, and appreciation.

Notable destinations: Tea lovers could plan an entire trip to China around tea, visiting oolong plantations in the Wuyi mountains, touring *pu-erh* factories in Yunnan Province, and shopping for teapots in the so-called pottery capital of Yixing. However, in big cities such as Beijing and Shanghai, keep an eye out for the "tea ceremony scam," where tourists are invited to sample teas at traditional Chinese tea houses and then asked to pay an exorbitant bill. Always ask about pricing up-front.

JAPAN'S MATCHA TEA CEREMONY

"Tea is naught but this:
First you heat the water,
Then you make the tea,
Then you drink it properly.
That is all you need to know."

—SEN NO RIKYŪ, SIXTEENTH-CENTURY TEA MASTER

A simple tearoom lined with tatami mats. Graceful rituals shared between the host and their guests. The unmistakable hue and taste of matcha green tea. These are just a few of the fundamentals of the Japanese tea ceremony—known as *chado*, or "The Way of Tea."

As in *gong fu cha* (see page 96), this ceremony features a special collection of tools, including a tea scoop called the *chashaku* and a ceramic tea bowl, or *chawan*. Of all the utensils, however, the most important tool is the *chasen*, a whisk carved from a single piece of bamboo. After placing two or three scoops of matcha powder into the *chawan*, the host then uses the *chasen* to stir the matcha with hot water—whisking the tea quickly back and forth until foam as frothy as a cappuccino has formed. When not in use, the *chasen* can be stored on a ceramic holder or whisk keeper called the *kusenaoshi*, which helps the whisk retain its curved shape.

In the sixteenth century, renowned tea master Sen no Rikyū established the four principles of the Japanese tea ceremony: harmony, tranquility, purity, and respect. These principles can be seen in each step of the ceremony and are still essential to the tradition today. The peaceful setting of the tea house itself emanates harmony and tranquility, as do the refined movements of the host. Respect is embodied by the many bows exchanged between the host and guests, as well as how guests must enter through a small, low door—just as the samurai themselves once did (see page 73). Finally, the principle of purity is evidenced during the host's ceremonial cleansing of the utensils, a significant step that happens before and after the matcha is prepared and served.

Notable destinations: While there are many places to experience a traditional ceremony in Tokyo, which hosts the Grand Tea Ceremony festival every autumn, an even more fitting tea destination in Japan is the former imperial capital of Kyoto, where ancient temples and tea houses abound. The famed tea-growing region of Uji—known as the birthplace of matcha—is also just half an hour from downtown Kyoto.

KOREA'S DARYE

"The Way of Tea knows no doors."

—VENERABLE HYO DANG, KOREAN TEA MASTER

Given China's status as the birthplace of tea and the greater awareness around the world of the Japanese tea ceremony, it's easy to see how Korea's centuries-old tea culture is usually overshadowed by those of its neighbors. And yet, while the traditional Korean tea ceremony known as *darye*, meaning "etiquette for tea," bears a strong resemblance to its Japanese counterpart—especially in the host's elegant, choreographed movements while preparing green tea for their guests—it also offers up some unique elements. Defining elements of this ceremony are the pale jade-colored celadon pottery used for brewing and serving, as well as the ritual of drinking your cup of tea in just three sips, as a means of truly focusing on the aromas and flavors of the tea and the experience of the ceremony.

Notable destinations: The county of Hadong is home to South Korea's first green tea plantation, dating back 1,200 years. The Hadong Green Tea Culture Center lets visitors take part in the tea roasting process and a tea ceremony.

TIBET'S *PO CHA*

*"The tea horse road is a long, long one;
it leads you all the way to heaven."*
—TRADITIONAL YUNNAN SONG

The more tea began to travel beyond China—along the Tea Horse Road (see page 15) and other ancient caravan routes—the more it was shaped by different cultures, according to the particular needs of each place. In Japan and Korea, monks consumed green tea as an aid for meditation practice, whereas Tibetans supplemented their meat-heavy diets with bricks of black tea, whose liquor provided nutrients and aided digestion. After boiling the tea for hours, they mixed it with yak butter, milk, and salt, creating Tibet's iconic butter tea known as *po cha*. Traditionally a wooden tea churn called a *chandong* was used to combine the mixture; today, an electric blender typically gets the job done.

Notable destinations: For your first taste of Tibet's national drink, head to the region's capital city of Lhasa and its myriad traditional tea houses. Many are located along Barkhor Street, which encircles the seventh-century Jokhang Temple and forms a sacred pilgrimage circuit known in Tibetan Buddhism as a *kora*.

RUSSIA'S ZAVARKA

"I say let the world go to hell,
  but I should always have my tea."
—FYODOR DOSTOYEVSKY, *NOTES FROM UNDERGROUND*

Russia's famed tea culture got its start in the seventeenth century, when tea began arriving from China by way of camel caravans. These convoys gave the Russian Caravan blend of black tea not only its name, but its characteristic smoky flavor, too—thanks to nightly campfires during the year-long journey.

What makes Russian tea distinct from other tea traditions is its manner of preparation and presentation. The key component is a tea urn known as a samovar, which in Russian loosely means "self-boiler." This unique and often incredibly decorative brewing device features a large cylinder in which water is boiled, plus a teapot that sits on top of the cylinder and is filled with a concentrated brew of tea called

zavarka. When it's time to serve, the tea is diluted with water, depending on the desired strength of each guest, and frequently sweetened with jam. So central has the samovar been in Russian hospitality that a popular expression refers to enjoying tea over a chat with friends as "having a sit by the samovar."

Notable destinations: Russia's coastal city of Sochi didn't just host the 2014 Olympic Games—it is also home to the northernmost tea-growing region in the world, due to Sochi's subtropical climate along the Black Sea; the Dagomys Tea Plantation offers guided tours and tastings. In Moscow, another memorable destination awaits tea lovers at the Perlov Tea House, whose intricate façade resembling a Chinese pagoda was commissioned by tea merchant Sergei Perlov in 1896.

TURKEY'S ÇAY

*"Conversations without tea are like
a night sky without the moon."*
—TURKISH FOLK SAYING

From the lively bazaars of Istanbul to the quietest village in Anatolia, there's hardly a corner of Turkey where you can't get a cup of strong black tea—or, as it's known in Turkish, *çay* (pronounced just like chai). Given that Turkey boasts the highest per-capita consumption of tea in the world—averaging seven pounds per person each year!—it's surprising to learn that tea found its stronghold in the country only recently, after World War I. Coffee had historically been the drink of choice in Turkey, but as the costs of importing coffee soared following the war, Turkey turned to black tea—both as a producer and consumer.

As tea became popular, Turkey looked to the Russians for brewing inspiration as well. Turkish *çay* is prepared using a samovar-like vessel called a *çaydanlık*, which looks like two silver teapots stacked together. Turkish tea ware is distinctive as well; instead of teacups, the beverage is served in small, tulip-shaped glasses, often with colorful, red-and-white saucers. Today, tea plays an intrinsic role in Turkish culture and hospitality—no matter the hour, endless rounds of *çay* are served to guests at every occasion, from leisurely meals to business meetings.

Notable destinations: Just across the Black Sea from Sochi is Turkey's prized tea-growing region, the hilly, northeastern province of Rize. For a glimpse of the province's lush tea plantations—and for truly breathtaking views over the city of Rize—head to the Ziraat Botanik Tea Garden. It's owned by Çaykur Tea, Turkey's largest, state-owned tea producer, and is also home to a tea research institute.

IRAN'S *CHAIKHANEHS*

Tea arrived in Iran in the fifteenth century thanks to another ancient route: the Silk Road. The relative ease of obtaining tea from China swiftly led to the drink's dominance over coffee in Iran, as well as to the rise of tea houses, known as *chaikhanehs*. Persian tea is brewed in a samovar, like Russian *zavarka*, and it's often sweetened. But rather than stirring granules into your cup, the tradition is to place a sugar cube or piece of yellow rock candy called *nabat* between your front teeth before taking a sip of tea.

Although the drink has been in Iran for centuries, the history of this country's tea production is much more recent, and it includes another fascinating tale of tea espionage. In 1899, an Iranian prince named Mohammad Mirza was serving as the country's ambassador to India. Just like China before them, the English closely guarded their new secrets of tea production in India. However, the prince was fluent in French, so, as if following in the footsteps of Robert Fortune (see page 17), he disguised himself as a French laborer, went to work on Indian tea plantations, and ultimately smuggled three thousand tea plants back to Iran—which, given his diplomatic immunity, went undetected by the British. Today, Mirza is known as the "father of Iranian tea."

Notable destinations: Tehran is home to countless *chaikhanehs* worth visiting, from the Azari Traditional Tea House to the tiny Haj Ali Darvish Teahouse in the Grand Bazaar—known as "the world's smallest tea house." Tea lovers can also head to Prince Mirza's native province of Gilan, along the Caspian Sea, which produces 90 percent of Iran's tea and is home to the National Tea Museum.

INDIA'S MASALA CHAI

India is not only home to more than one billion people—it's also the birthplace of the spice-infused concoction known as masala chai (*masala* literally means "spice" in Hindi). In some ways, chai has ancient origins. Early Ayurvedic texts prescribed medicinal drinks featuring many of the spices found in chai today, such as cardamom, cinnamon, ginger, and black pepper.

In other ways, however, chai is still very new. When the British began growing tea in India in the mid-1800s, tea was expensive and slow to be embraced by Indians. It was only in the early twentieth century that the Indian Tea Association, a trade group that protects the interests of tea producers and laborers, made a concerted effort to build domestic demand for tea. Although the association promoted the English way of taking tea, Indian tea vendors (known as *chai wallahs*) drew on their own long tradition of preparing drinks using aromatic seasonings and created the singular sweet, milky mix of black tea and spices now beloved across India. Chai lattes have also become popular in coffee shops around the world; however, they often use ready-made chai syrups, which don't always capture the rich and nuanced flavors of the traditional drink.

Notable destinations: Tea lovers are spoiled for choice in India, where tea fields lay in nearly every direction— including Darjeeling in the Himalayas, low-lying Assam along the Brahmaputra River, and Nilgiri in the south, where beautiful tea estates hug the slopes of the Blue Mountains.

PAKISTAN'S *NOON CHAI*

Made from green tea leaves, Pakistan's *noon chai* is the lesser-known cousin of masala chai—but by no means is it any less delicious or memorable. Also known as Kashmiri chai in honor of its roots, this tea is named after the Kashmiri word for salt, *noon*, because *noon chai* is traditionally salty, not sweet. It also features another unusual ingredient for tea—a pinch of baking soda that gives the drink its signature vivid pink hue. Finally, a few spices such as cardamom and cinnamon are added to the rose-colored creation, which is then topped with a dusting of ground almonds and pistachios. *Noon chai* is often served at special occasions and weddings, especially during the brisk winters of Kashmir.

Notable destinations: You don't have to be invited to a Kashmiri wedding in order to taste an authentic iteration of the region's acclaimed pink tea. Just across the border from India, head to Pakistan's twin cities of Islamabad and Rawalpindi. Tea stalls abound with sweetened versions of *noon chai*, but a classic Kashmiri restaurant called the Dilbar Hotel offers some of the only salty tea found in the two cities.

MOROCCO'S MINT TEA

Long before tea came to be ubiquitous across Morocco and other countries in Northern Africa, Moroccans prepared herbal infusions, or tisanes—the most popular of which was spearmint. When the Crimean War broke out in 1853, the British began transporting gunpowder green tea from China to Morocco, where it was soon added to the traditional sweet mint infusions.

Morocco's world-famous mint tea is now celebrated as the national beverage, and it plays a key role in rituals of hospitality, both in friendship and business. The tools of a traditional Moroccan tea ceremony (known as *atai*) are especially noteworthy—including the silver teapot, or *bred*, and colorful tea glasses called *keesan*—as is the practice of pouring this tea into the glass from a great height. This technique is visually exciting and produces a foam on the surface of the tea, signaling that it was adequately brewed.

Notable destinations: For an opulent tea experience, head to Casablanca and visit Wright 1856, the country's first luxury tea house that today includes a tea museum.

BRITAIN'S AFTERNOON TEA

"There are few hours in life more agreeable than the hour dedicated to the ceremony known as afternoon tea."

—HENRY JAMES, *THE PORTRAIT OF A LADY*

We've all felt those twinges of hunger between lunch and dinner; in 1840, an English duchess named Anna Maria Russell decided to do something about what she described as "that sinking feeling." She began to request a pot of tea to her room in the late afternoon, along with cakes and some bread and butter. It didn't take long before she invited her high-society friends to join her, and by the 1880s, their new ritual had become a fixture in drawing rooms across the country.

The tradition of afternoon tea still lives on today, especially in the English tea service. The tea pot, tray, and sugar-and-creamer set are typically made from porcelain, though silver may be used in formal settings. The typical centerpiece is a three-tiered stand, featuring a selection of savories, scones, and sweets. That's also the order in which the food should be eaten, starting with savories and finger sandwiches on the lowest tier and ending with sweets on the top.

Given these rich foods, robust black teas such as Assam, Ceylon, and Darjeeling are traditionally served at afternoon tea, as well as the classic British blend of Earl Grey. Herbal infusions such as chamomile and mint often make an appearance, too.

Notable destinations: There's no shortage of places in London to experience afternoon tea, from luxury hotels like Claridges and the Ritz to high-end department stores such as Fortnum & Mason. Elsewhere in England, Bettys Café Tea Room has been a Yorkshire institution since 1919, and the southwestern counties of Devon and Cornwall each claim to be the home of cream tea—a popular take on afternoon tea featuring scones accompanied by clotted cream and jam.

NEW ZEALAND'S HIGH TEA

"Go into their homes and tea appears as if by magic."

—CRAWFORD SOMERSET, *LITTLEDENE:*
A NEW ZEALAND RURAL COMMUNITY

Just as monks once carried tea with them across Asia, tea also arrived in New Zealand thanks to travelers—beginning with sealers and whalers in the 1700s and continuing with British missionaries in the 1800s. Given that New Zealand was initially a British colony, it's little surprise that tea caught on as quickly as it did there, as well as related rituals such as high tea.

Lovers of English afternoon tea will recognize many elements in New Zealand's high tea, from porcelain teacups and saucers to three-tiered stands overflowing with sandwiches, scones, and sweets. However, some establishments have put their own spin on the tradition; for example, the Heritage Hotel in Auckland offers a vegan high tea, and Zealong Tea Estate (read more below) serves up Asian-inspired eats such as miso tofu to accompany their organic, New Zealand–grown teas.

Notable destinations: Tea lovers can sip their way right across New Zealand, starting at Auckland's original tea kiosk in Wintergarden Pavilion and ending with traditional high tea at Larnach Castle in Dunedin.

But the true can't-miss tea destination is Zealong, the only commercial tea estate in New Zealand, founded in 1996. Tea tours include a guided walk through the estate's gardens, where a series of larger-than-life bronze statues tells the "New Zealand tea story." Statues include our patron saint of tea, Lu Yu (see page 37), as well as tea porters bearing their loads along the ancient Tea Horse Road.

AMERICA'S SOUTHERN SWEET TEA

"Sweet tea is the house wine of the South."

—DOLLY PARTON IN *STEEL MAGNOLIAS*

Few things are more definitively Southern than a glass of sweetened iced tea, especially when paired with other regional essentials like fried chicken or barbecue. This style is typically made with standard black tea bags, and it is brewed hot, sweetened with sugar, and then chilled.

A popular origin story dates iced tea to the 1904 World's Fair in St. Louis, Missouri—where the sweltering heat inspired one vendor to run his hot tea through iced lead pipes. But there's plenty of proof that the sweet concoction has helped people stay cool since the nineteenth century. The first recipe for iced tea was published in the 1879 community cookbook *Housekeeping in Old Virginia*, edited by Marion Cabell Tyree; its suggestions for adding sugar and "a squeeze of lemon" are still followed today.

Notable destinations: For a taste of the South's iconic brew, head to the "Birthplace of Sweet Tea," Summerville,

South Carolina. Attend its annual Sweet Tea Festival, held every September, and pay homage to the World's Largest Iced Tea, a record-breaking attraction featuring a 15-foot-tall replica mason jar. The Charleston Tea Plantation is also just an hour south of Summerville; there, you can tour the only large-scale commercial tea plantation in the United States.

SOUTH AMERICA'S YERBA MATE

Farther south in the Americas, another form and flavor of tea reigns king: yerba mate. Because its leaves come from the holly family, mate isn't technically a true tea. However, it has been consumed since the pre-Columbian era—most widely in Paraguay, Argentina, Uruguay, and southern Brazil. Mate is distinct in nearly every way from other teas and tisanes, renowned for both its bitter taste and for the components used to prepare it—a hollow, gourd-shaped cup; a metal straw called a bombilla; and a thermos of hot water for refilling the gourd and brewing multiple infusions of the leaves.

Most striking of all, mate is a deeply communal and ritualized drink. In a group setting, one person—referred to in Spanish as the *cebador*—assumes the role of serving the mate, passing a single gourd and straw around the group. Another ritual states that you should

only say "thank you" to the *cebador* when you don't want another round of tea. Just as in Turkey or Morocco, mate ultimately embodies the close-knit communities and welcoming spirit found in cultures across South America.

Notable destinations: Given mate's status as a social drink, it isn't typically available to order at restaurants in South America. That said, visiting tea lovers still have a chance to taste mate in the Argentine capital of Buenos Aires, where a handful of steakhouses (known as *parrillas*) offer yerba mate on their menus—including Las Cabras, La Cholita, and Cumaná.

HONG KONG'S PANTYHOSE TEA

Thanks to its fusion of Chinese heritage and British colonial past, Hong Kong has long been known for its "East meets West" culture and cuisine. One of the greatest examples of this is Hong Kong–style milk tea, which evolved in the 1950s from the English tradition of drinking black tea with milk and sugar.

The defining feature of this tea is the use of a unique cloth filter for straining the leaves, whose long, socklike shape has led to unconventional nicknames for the drink: pantyhose tea, or silk stocking milk tea. The strong, fragrant brew of black tea is combined with condensed or evaporated milk—a common practice in newer Asian tea traditions, given that canned milk has a longer shelf life than fresh milk and is more readily available. This method of making milk tea has even been officially listed as an Intangible Cultural Heritage item in Hong Kong.

Notable destinations: For a quintessential taste of pantyhose tea, head to one of Hong Kong's greasy-spoon-style diners known as *cha chaan teng*, which literally means "tea restaurant." Lan Fong Yuen is one of the most famous and is said to have been the birthplace of pantyhose tea more than fifty years ago.

MALAYSIA'S *TEH TARIK*

Just like its neighbor Singapore to the south, Malaysia is home to a fascinating mix of cultures. Even its signature pulled tea, *teh tarik*, is a hybrid of traditions. When Indian Muslim immigrants arrived in the twentieth century as migrant workers, they brought their love of chai (see page 110) with them. To save money, they used low-grade tea dust sourced from Chinese tea plantations, whose strong, bitter-tasting brew was improved by adding condensed or evaporated milk. The result is now considered Malaysia's national beverage.

However, the real secret of *teh tarik* isn't *what* goes into the tea, but *how* it's prepared. Before vendors serve the hot drink, they pour—or "pull"—the tea back and forth between two stainless-steel pitchers, which aerates the liquid and gives the tea a rich, frothy texture. There's an art to pulling tea and a serious element of showmanship, as vendors race to pour the tea from greater and greater distances before audiences of customers and passersby. Some even take part in organized contests—only in Malaysia is tea a competitive sport!

Notable destinations: Tea lovers in Malaysia will be hard-pressed to find a coffee shop or food stall (known as a *mamak*) that doesn't serve *teh tarik*, so prevalent is pulled tea across the country. For a glimpse into the production side of Malaysia's tea culture, head north out of Kuala Lumpur into the picturesque Cameron Highlands. Formerly a hill station under British colonial rule, the region offers a plethora of tea fields to visit, including BOH Tea Estate and Cameron Bharat Plantations.

THAILAND'S *CHA YEN*

One surefire way to beat Bangkok's balmy heat—not to mention the country's equally spicy cuisine—is a refreshing glass of Thai iced tea. It's also known as *cha yen,* which literally means "cold tea," and it starts with a strongly brewed Assam or Ceylon tea. An especially popular tea blend used in *cha yen* is the Thai brand Cha Dra Muer, which contains the yellow no. 6 food coloring, an unusual ingredient that helps give this beverage its signature bright orange hue.

Once the tea is brewed, it is poured hot over crushed ice, along with generous amounts of sugar, sweetened condensed milk, and evaporated milk (Carnation brand cans are a ubiquitous presence at *cha yen* stalls). The final concoction may not be the healthiest tea you'll ever drink, but its sweet taste and creamy texture are perfectly suited to keeping you cool.

Notable destinations: You don't have to search hard for Thai iced tea in Bangkok—*cha yen* is a staple of the city's celebrated street food culture and sidewalk stalls. Farther north in Thailand, the misty highlands surrounding Chiang Mai and Chiang Rai are home to a number of tea fields, including 101 Tea Plantation, whose oolong won first place at the 2004 World Tea Festival.

TAIWAN'S BUBBLE TEA

Although oolongs are one of Taiwan's specialties, the island might be even more famous for introducing the world to another twist on tea: bubble tea, also known as boba or pearl milk tea. In the 1980s, an enterprising tea house owner named Liu Han-Chieh started serving chilled tea after a trip to Japan during which he saw coffee being served cold. One of his managers took the idea a step further, by adding marble-sized balls of tapioca starch (or *fen yuan*) to her iced tea—and the sweet, chewy outcome was an instant hit.

Today, the original pearl milk tea still features creamy iced tea, syrup, and black tapioca pearls—always shaken to a froth and served with an extra-wide straw big enough for slurping up the pearls. But as the boba craze continues taking the world by storm, there's no end to new flavors and variations to try. Tropical fruit flavors are especially popular, such as mango, honeydew, and passionfruit. Adventurous bubble tea lovers should visit Wang Tea Egg in Taiwan, where the milk tea is served with a hard-boiled egg that has been cooked in tea.

Notable destinations: Taiwan's capital city of Taipei seems to offer a bubble tea shop at every street corner and night market—including chains such as 50 Lan, Yi Fang, and Tiger Sugar. True boba fanatics should head south to the city of Taichung. Chun Shui Tang Cultural Tea House is known as the "birthplace of bubble tea," and its location inside the National Taiwan Museum of Fine Arts offers DIY bubble tea-making classes, so you can get a hands-on taste of this iconic drink.

TEA
PARTIES

HOW TO HOST AN AFTERNOON TEA FOR ADULTS

Anytime's a good time for tea, but certain occasions call for something special. Whether you're planning a birthday party, bridal shower, or simply a get-together with good friends, get your *Downton Abbey* on and follow these tips for your next afternoon tea. Pinkies up, everyone! (Want to serve some adults-only beverages at your gatherings? See page 140.)

CHOOSE A THEME

Giving your afternoon tea a theme will add a little extra flair to the event, and it could even inspire creative menus and decorations. Here are some fun themes to consider.

- Literary: Books and tea are a match made in heaven, so what could be better than a literary tea party? British classic literature is an especially good source of inspiration, such as *Alice in Wonderland*, *Pride and Prejudice*, and the Chronicles of Narnia series (Turkish delight, anyone?).

- **Holiday:** From Valentine's Day to Mother's Day to Christmas, the calendar is full of ideas to give your tea a seasonal twist.

- **Geographic:** For more themes, look no further than the myriad of tea traditions across the world. An Indian tea might feature masala chai and savory samosas, while a Japanese-inspired afternoon could pair matcha green tea with traditional bean sweets known as *wagashi*. (See the global tea traditions discussed on pages 96–126 for ideas.)

DESIGN YOUR MENU

Full afternoon tea calls for three courses: savories, scones, and sweets, which are typically eaten in that order. Dainty-yet-delicious finger sandwiches are a must for your first savory course—consider filling the bottom tier of your tea stand with these tasty offerings (just don't forget to trim the crusts).

- **Tea sandwich classics:** You can't go wrong with trustworthy combos such as cucumber and dill, smoked salmon and cream cheese, or egg salad and dijon mustard.

- **Spice things up:** For an afternoon tea with a kick, serve up spicy pimento cheese sandwiches or curried chicken salad sandwiches with cranberries (this works well in lettuce cups, if you want to serve a gluten-free option).

- **Dress (your sandwich) to impress:** If you want to seriously turn heads, take some thinly sliced radishes or prosciutto, shape them into roses, and place them on top of open-faced sandwiches.

DO-IT-YOURSELF TEA BLENDS

In addition to serving classic afternoon teas such as Darjeeling or Earl Grey, you could also mix things up (literally!) by inviting guests to create their own tea blends at your party. All you'll need are tea filter bags, loose-leaf teas for the base of each blend, and a few of the following ingredients:

- **Dried flowers:** chamomile, rose hips, hibiscus petals

- **Fruit:** candied pineapple or mango pieces, dried orange slices, shredded coconut

- **Fresh herbs:** lavender buds, mint leaves, lemongrass stalks

- **Whole spices:** star anise, cloves, green cardamom pods

Depending on the time of year of your party, consider blending green teas with fruit for a summery twist; black teas and spices make for a delightfully autumnal homemade chai. Loose-leaf rooibos makes a great base for a caffeine-free blend. Aim for three to four components per blend, using around a teaspoon or two total for each filter bag, and don't forget to have guests christen their custom tea blend with a name.

HOW TO THROW A TEA PARTY FOR CHILDREN

The wonderful thing about tea is that unlike with beverages such as coffee or wine, you don't have to wait for children to reach a certain age before you can share it with them—tea is a drink for the whole family to enjoy! The following hands-on ideas can help you get even the youngest tea lovers involved.

DIY SUGAR CUBES

Homemade sugar cubes are a fun way to bring color and whimsy to a children's tea party—but be warned: after you've made them once, there's no going back to plain white sugar cubes.

Supplies needed:

- Granulated sugar
- Water
- Food coloring
- Flavoring extracts, such as mint, almond, or vanilla
- Silicone candy molds

Using a tablespoon of water for every cup of sugar, mix the sugar and water in a bowl using a spoon (aim for a crumbly texture that reminds you of wet sand). You should also add a few drops of food coloring at this stage, as well as a bit of flavoring extract.

Firmly press the sugar mixture into the candy molds, before letting them dry overnight at room temperature; the next morning, the sugar cubes should be set enough to remove from the molds.

Tip: Because the sugar cubes need to dry overnight, make them in advance of the tea party. Or, if you'd like to help children make their own cubes at the party, they could each take home a mold of freshly made cubes as a party favor.

CREATE YOUR OWN TEA TAGS

One of the best things about tea bags are tea tags—the little paper tab attached with string that helps you remove the bag after steeping. Herbal tea brand Yogi Tea is even famous for putting inspirational quotes and messages on their tags. Here's how kids can create their own personalized tea tags.

Supplies needed:

- Colored cardstock or construction paper
- Scissors or paper punches
- Art supplies such as markers and colored pencils
- Glue sticks

Cut out several matching shapes from the cardstock using scissors. You could also use a large paper punch; Fiskars has models in many shapes, including a heart, star, and flower. This could even make your tea tags coordinate nicely with your DIY sugar cubes, depending on what shape molds you used.

Have kids unleash their creative magic on the cut paper, adding their own decorations on one side of each tag. Then take a pair of shapes and glue the undecorated sides together to make a tea tag. You can either remove the existing tag from a store-bought tea bag and glue your new tag to it, or, better yet, make your own loose-leaf tea blends (see page 132) using tea sachets, which often come with a built-in drawstring for attaching a tea tag. Kids can enjoy their personalized tea bags at the party or take them home as favors.

EDIBLE COOKIE SPOONS

In lieu of traditional silver teaspoons, who wouldn't love to decorate their own edible cookie spoon? These delicious and interactive treats will make your tea party one to remember.

Supplies needed:

- Shortbread cookie ingredients (typically butter, sugar, flour, and salt, but check your favorite recipe)

- Spoon-shaped cookie cutter

- Flavorings as desired, such as honey or vanilla extract

- Decorative toppings such as sprinkles, chocolate, etc.

A day or two before the party, prepare your favorite shortbread recipe, add any desired flavorings, and use a spoon-shaped cookie cutter to cut out the spoons from the dough, and bake according to the recipe. At the party, set out bowls of decorations and have children adorn their cookie spoons, dipping them in chocolate and giving them a healthy dusting of sprinkles or sugar pearls before stirring their tea.

A BASIC RECIPE FOR SCONES

Whether you're hosting adults or children—or simply enjoying a cuppa by yourself—these scones are a perfect companion for your favorite tea. This recipe makes 8 scones.

Ingredients

- 3 cups all-purpose flour
- ½ cup granulated sugar
- 5 teaspoons baking powder
- ½ teaspoon salt
- ¾ cup butter, cut into ½-inch cubes and chilled in the fridge or freezer
- 1 beaten egg
- 1 cup buttermilk or whole milk (or half-and-half, for even creamier scones)

Directions

Before getting started, preheat your oven to 400°F (200°C), and line a baking sheet with parchment paper or grease it with cooking spray.

In a large bowl, combine the flour, sugar, baking powder, and salt. Add the butter, which should be cold (i.e., taken straight from the fridge or freezer). Keeping the butter cold before adding it ensures that the scone dough has small pieces of butter in it, which will then melt during baking and leave behind little pockets of air, giving the scones their signature height and fluffy texture.

In a separate bowl combine the egg and milk, and then gradually add them to the flour mixture, stirring to incorporate. Place the dough on a floured surface and lightly knead it—overkneading can lead to tough scones—and then use a rolling pin to roll it out into a circle measuring between ½ inch and 1 inch thick. Using a knife, cut the circle into 8 wedges and arrange them on the prepared baking sheet.

Bake the scones for 15 minutes, or until risen and golden brown. Note: At their best, scones are melt-in-your-mouth soft, but they can also be temperamental. If you're planning to make them for the first time for a tea party, it could pay off to do a test run before the big day.

TEA COCKTAILS

The earliest versions of American iced tea were often spiked green tea punches. In fact, the nineteenth-century Regent's Punch called for Champagne, brandy, rum, *and* arrack. In honor of tea's roots in the U.S., try out one (or more) of the following tea cocktails at your next afternoon tea, or experiment with mixing your own tea-infused tipples.

If you're brewing tea for use in cocktails, make it stronger than you normally would (some recipes call for tea concentrates, which typically use 2 tea bags per 3 fluid ounces of water). Apart from the Chai Hot Toddy, the recipes below call for tea that's been chilled before combining with the other cocktail ingredients.

- Earl Grey Martini: The citrusy notes of bergamot in Earl Grey make this tea blend a natural fit for gin-based drinks, such as a Tom Collins or gin martini. *Calls for 1½ fluid ounces of strong Earl Grey tea.*

- Mint Tea Mojito: Mint is a staple ingredient in many cocktails, so why not mint tea? Mix it with rum for a mojito, or, if you're feeling especially Southern, with bourbon for a mint julep. *Calls for 4 fluid ounces of mint tea.*

- **Hibiscus Margarita:** Give your margaritas a pop of color and tang with the hot pink liquor of hibiscus tea; you could also substitute it for cranberry juice in a classic Cosmopolitan. *Calls for 4 fluid ounces of hibiscus tea.*

- **Chai Hot Toddy:** Featuring whisky, lemon, and honey, a traditional hot toddy is garnished with spices such as cinnamon sticks, star anise, or cloves. Chai is a perfect addition to this cozy, warming cocktail. *Calls for 8 fluid ounces of chai.*

RESOURCES

ETHICAL TEA GUIDE

Around the world, tea growers and pickers (who are predominantly women) are notoriously underpaid. The following companies sell organic, certified fair trade teas that help provide their workers with better wages and working conditions.

- Arbor Teas
  arborteas.com
- Equal Exchange
  shop.equalexchange.coop
- Guayakí
  guayaki.com
- Hampstead Tea
  hampsteadtea.com
- The London Tea Company
  londontea.co.uk
- Numi Organic Tea
  numitea.com
- Organic India
  organicindiausa.com

FURTHER READING

Books

A History of Tea: The Life and Times of the World's Favorite Beverage
by Laura C. Martin

The Tea Enthusiast's Handbook: A Guide to Enjoying the World's Best Teas
by Mary Lou Heiss and Robert J. Heiss

A Little Tea Book: All the Essentials from Leaf to Cup
by Sebastian Beckwith and Caroline Paul

Tea Sommelier: A Step-by-Step Guide
by François-Xavier Delmas and Mathias Minet

Websites

- American Specialty Tea Alliance
  specialtyteaalliance.org
- Tea Epicure
  teaepicure.com
- Discovering Tea: A Tea Traveller's Blog
  discoveringtea.com
- Mei Leaf
  meileaf.com

ACKNOWLEDGMENTS

*"Tea is a work of art and needs a master
hand to bring out its noblest qualities."*

—OKAKURA KAKUZO, *THE BOOK OF TEA*

There were many master hands who helped bring out the best in this book. First and foremost, I'm grateful to Jhanteigh Kupihea for approaching me with this rewarding project. Thank you as well to Jane Morley, Rebecca Gyllenhaal, and the entire team at Quirk Books, and to Lucy Engelman for her beautiful illustrations.

In further gratitude, many thanks to my agent Rachel Sussman, cofounder of Chalberg & Sussman, and to my incredible family, dear friends, and community around the world—especially Cara, for being the best sounding board and anchor a friend could hope for. Thank you also to Victoria Rodríguez, tea sommelier and owner of Reencontraté in Montevideo, Uruguay, for sharing her endless tea wisdom with me.

Finally, to my partner, best friend, and resident yerba mate expert José. Thank you for your unconditional love, for being such a fierce supporter of my dreams (as I'll always be of yours), and for all the mates we shared as this book came to life.